You Hold the Keys to Your Child's Character

You Hold the Keys to Your Child's Character

Praying for Your Child's Christian Growth

Lynda Hunter, Ed.D.

SERVANT PUBLICATIONS
ANN ARBOR, MICHIGAN

Vine Books is an imprint of Servant Publications especially designed to serve evangelical Christians.

Published by Servant Publications
P.O. Box 8617
Ann Arbor, Michigan 48107

Cover design: Alicia Vazquez
Cover illustrations: © Shirley V. Beckes / Artville. Used by permission.

98 99 00 10 9 8 7 6 5 4 3 2 1

Printed in the United States of America
ISBN 1-56955-086-7

LIBRARY OF CONGRESS CATALOGING-IN-PUBLICATION DATA

Hunter, Lynda.
You hold the key to your child's character : praying for your child's Christian character / Lynda Hunter.
p. cm.
ISBN 1-56955-086-7 (alk. paper)
1. Parents—Prayer-books and devotions—English. 2. Children—Religious life. 3. Virtues. 4. Devotional calendars. I. Title.
BV4529.H86 1998
242'.62—dc21 98-29416
CIP

Contents

Preface

One Saturday afternoon in my childhood, my family and I stopped by the five-and-ten store on our way to the church my dad pastored. Mom went in with my brother and three sisters, but across the street, banners and a crowd of people announced the grand opening of a new bank. Dad's curiosity and my ten-year-old wonder drew us over, with me holding his hand securely.

Refreshments, door prizes, and friendly faces abounded. As Dad and I made our way through the crowd, I strained to see above tall shoulders in front of me. Then, suddenly, I spied a man with a treasure chest. "Just pick the right key to open the lock," he said, "and all the money you can gather in your hands will be yours."

The possibilities took my breath away. As the second oldest of what would eventually be eight children, I knew my dad's paycheck as a mail carrier barely covered our necessities.

We took our place in line. Dad looked like a giant standing in front of me. I bowed my head as we moved closer to the box holding the keys. "God," I whispered, "would You help my dad choose the right key?"

My prayer concluded, I watched Dad's big hand stretch across the tray of choices. Finally, his thumb and first finger came together as he selected a key and lifted it from the box.

The man let me take one, too. With the thumb of my left hand, I pressed hard against the cold, gray key cradled in my right palm. I pushed and twisted it harder as Dad's turn at the chest drew near, and I repeated my simple prayer.

His chance finally came. Dad aimed his key at the lock and stuck it in the hole. I could feel the sweat on my forehead as his hand turned. Silence. Then he looked down at me and shook his head.

Disappointment overwhelmed me as he turned to walk away. *Why didn't God answer my prayer?* I wondered.

Lost in thought, at first I didn't hear the man's voice drawing my attention back to the chest. "Your turn, honey," he said.

I lifted my limp hand and placed the key into the lock. I turned it to the right, and suddenly, the lock opened! The man lifted the lid, revealing mounds of dimes, nickels, quarters, and a few half dollars. My eyes grew bigger than the biggest of them. I took a deep breath, gathered all I could hold in my hands, pulled the money quickly toward my chest, and moved hurriedly across the floor to where Dad stood. Before long I had counted $2.97, $2.98, $2.99, $3.00. After adding in a few more cents, I looked up and said, "Let's go get some ice cream."

I don't remember what kind of treat everyone got, but I do still remember the family's unexpected delight and my pride in being the one to provide it.

Many years later, I became a mom. Too soon, I sent my children off to school, where strangers took over most of their day. I needed someone to protect and nurture them when I couldn't be around. I hadn't practiced praying on my own through my growing-up years, so I never really thought about praying for my children on my own. I thought about calling Mom and Dad for prayer support. But they lived far away, and Dad had grown gravely ill. I looked to people in my church, but they had problems of their own. Who could help me?

Suddenly, I could almost feel the cold, gray key pressed against the palm of my hand once more. I could still imagine Dad and many others bigger than me, standing way ahead. I had assumed they held just the right keys. Their experience and wisdom, as well as their hand spans, measured much larger than mine. I had never even thought to ask God to help me find the key myself.

But today, with no one else to turn to, I do ask God. "Please, give me the key to answered prayers," I plead. "Tell me what to request for my children."

Many more days have passed. Many more problems have arisen. Many more people have let me down as I have searched for answers. But I don't panic anymore. I have learned that the key will always be there in my hand through my relationship with Jesus Christ. "Ask and it will be given to you; seek and you will find; knock and the door will be opened to you" (Matthew 7:7).

Because of that promise, I can write this book with confidence. Through asking, seeking, and knocking, we can go to God for everything that concerns our children, including the character qualities this book describes. Together, we'll explore thirty-one godly traits to ask for and how to ask for them—one for each day of the month. May the words in these pages be one more reminder that the key of prayer will open the treasures of all God has in store, especially for our kids.

A Word to Parents:

Your prayers can have a powerful effect on the virtue in your child's heart. The role of a Christian parent is not unlike that of the high priest in the Old Testament. He went into the Holy of Holies, offered sacrifices, and talked to God about issues that concerned the people.

In Exodus 28, God told Moses how to dress the high priest—his brother Aaron—in holy garments. On his clothes he mounted precious stones representing the twelve tribes of Israel. These stones would signify bringing the people's needs before God: "Whenever Aaron enters the Holy Place, he will bear the names of the sons of Israel over his heart on the breastpiece of decision as a continuing memorial before the Lord.... Thus Aaron will always bear the means of making decision for the Israelites" (Exodus 28:29-30).

When the office of the high priest became corrupt, God used prophets to speak to His people. Then, God sent His Son, Jesus Christ. We read in Hebrews 1:1 that at that time we gained direct access to God through Jesus. We are able to go before God and intercede on behalf of our children.

As we do that, once again, we can look to the high priest's example to show us how. The priest's robe is described in Exodus 39:22-26. On the hem of the blue robe hung strands of yarn formed like the pomegranate fruit. The pomegranates acted as pads between hand-beaten gold bells that chimed together in perfect harmony. The soft yarn of the pomegranates kept the bells from striking each other in discord.

Author C. Paul Willis, in his book *Bells and Pomegranates,* says that this alternating bell and pomegranate configuration on the priest's robe could be likened to the gifts and fruit of the Holy Spirit in our lives.

The gifts are listed in 1 Corinthians 12:8-10: "To one there is given through the Spirit the message of wisdom, to another the message of knowledge ... to another faith ... to another gifts of healing ... to another miraculous powers, to another prophecy."

It's easy to see that our children are gifted, and we should pray for God's guidance in these areas of their lives. But it's not quite so easy to see that we should also pray for fruit, or virtues, to develop. In Galatians 5:22-23, we read about the fruit of the Spirit. This fruit depicts certain character qualities that we can develop in our growth as children of God. "But the fruit of the Spirit is love, joy, peace, patience, kindness, goodness, faithfulness, gentleness and self-control."

If we have the most talented son in the world, but he lacks integrity or compassion or humility, his gifts will be wasted. The Bible tells us: "If I speak in the tongues of men and of angels, but have not love, I am only a resounding gong or a clanging cymbal. If I have the gift of ... all knowledge ... but have not love, I am nothing. If I give all I possess ... and surrender my body to the flames, but have not love, I gain nothing" (1 Corinthians 13:1-3).

While much is heard these days about virtues and their importance, little is said about the importance of prayer in gaining them. I believe we parents hold the key to unlocking these valuable character qualities in our children, and that key is prayer.

Virtue's Pathway

We don't like to acknowledge that virtues are developed through hardship: "But we also rejoice in our sufferings, because we know that suffering produces perseverance; perseverance, character; and character, hope. And hope does not disappoint us, because God has poured out his love into our hearts by the Holy Spirit, whom he has given us" (Romans 5:3-5).

The trials, tribulations, and temptations our children will encounter can make or break them. We can be on our knees praying that these hardships will make them strong and foster in them godly character qualities. But exactly how do we do this?

Promises for Prayer

First, we need to commit to memory what the Bible has to say about prayer. Then it's like going to the bank, putting your passbook on the counter, and asking to withdraw funds. We know what God tells us about prayer. We speak the words He speaks, and we withdraw the answers He gives. Begin by memorizing scriptures such as the ones below:

- "Without faith it is impossible to please God, because anyone who comes to him must believe that he exists and that he rewards those who earnestly seek him" (Hebrews 11:6).

- "When you ask, you do not receive, because you ask with wrong motives" (James 4:3).

- "If two of you on earth agree about anything you ask for, it will be done for you by My Father in heaven. For where two or three come together in My name, there am I with them" (Matthew 18:19-20).

- "The Father will give you whatever you ask in My name" (John 15:16).

- "If you remain in Me and My words [the Bible] remain in you, ask whatever you wish, and it will be given you" (John 15:7).

Five-Step Praying

Powerful things happen when we lift our concerns to the throne of God Almighty. Because of prayer's importance, Satan fights us every step of the way with busyness, exhaustion, and ignorance about its value and how to do it.

Prayer is something we can learn to do better. In Luke 11, one of Jesus disciples said to Him, "Lord, teach us to pray" (v. 1). Jesus' gave all His followers a model through what we call "The Lord's Prayer". The King James Version of His model provides us with five steps to intercede for our children:

1. REVERE
"Our Father which art in heaven, Hallowed be Thy name."

All prayer should begin with revering the name of God: "Enter His gates with thanksgiving and His courts with praise" (Psalm 100:4). When we do that, we acknowledge God for who He is and what He's able to perform. Revering God also elevates us above circumstances to encounter the God who created both heaven and earth: "And God raised us up with Christ and seated us with Him in the heavenly realms in Christ Jesus" (Ephesians 2:6).

Singing hymns is one way to accomplish this. I have yet to sing songs of praise and worship without lifting my eyes past the immediate onto the bigger view of things. I play Christian music in my home whenever possible, and sometimes I open an old hymnbook—often just reading the words instead of singing them.

To revere God, just tell Him how much you love Him and how magnificent He is. He'll know what you mean and will draw you to Himself.

2. RELEASE
"Thy kingdom come. Thy will be done, as in heaven, so in earth."

When we pray for God's kingdom and His will, we submit and acknowledge that God is over all things and we can do nothing apart from Him. We also choose to leave behind an earthly perspective and instead lay all our concerns and circumstances at His throne.

Why seek His will? My life is filled with prayers I'm glad He didn't answer the way I wanted at the time: a certain boy to ask me out for a date in my youth or a particular job when I grew older. I have learned, instead, to seek God's will on certain matters and then pray in that direction.

God's will is often hard to determine. But there are two things we can be sure of while searching for the mind of God.

First, God never contradicts His Word. If He says something one place in Scripture, He won't refute it someplace else.

Second, Jesus left us the Holy Spirit to comfort and guide us. "We do not know what we ought to pray for, but the Spirit Himself intercedes for us with groans that words cannot express. And He Who searches our hearts knows the mind of the Spirit, because the Spirit intercedes for the saints in accordance with God's will" (Romans 8:26-27). We have an interpreter—one who knows the language. The Holy Spirit knows the mind of God and also lives inside the willing heart. That helps us when we ask for the will of God to be revealed to us.

Become familiar with what Scripture says about the area in which you seek His will, then pray for the Holy Spirit to guide you in the right direction. Though answers may not seem forthcoming, we know God's promise for us: "This is the confidence we have in approaching God: that if we ask anything according to His will, He hears us. And if we know that He hears us—whatever we ask—we know that we have what we asked of Him" (1 John 5:14-15).

Reading the Bible acquaints you not only with the mind of God, but also with your rights as a child of God. If you remain in me and my words remain in you," Jesus said, "ask whatever you wish, and it will be given you" (John 15:7).

When I'm seeking God's will, I find a scripture that I claim as my own for a particular situation. Then I pray that verse, inserting the person's name or the circumstance for which I'm praying. I invite the Holy Spirit to show me how to pray. And I pray with confidence.

3. REQUEST
"Give us day by day our daily bread."

Once I'm confident I have discovered God's will through Scripture and the Holy Spirit, I approach the throne boldly for my needs (see Hebrews 4:16). "Give us day by day our daily bread" reflects just that—a request for provision. God promises He will supply all our needs according to His glorious riches (see Philippians 4:19). Coming to Him in this way reminds us how totally dependent we are on Him. It gives God great pleasure to give to His children.

4. REPENT
"And forgive us our sins; for we also forgive every one that is indebted to us."

Praying with unconfessed sin present in our lives is like talking on the phone and encountering static: Our message won't get across. "Your iniquities have separated you from your God; your sins have hidden His face from you" (Isaiah

59:2). Each time we come before the throne of God, we should be sure that nothing lies between us and Him, seeking His cleansing when we discover sin. That sin may be in the form of things we've said or done, like offending someone. Or it may be a sin of omission, such as neglecting to pray or failing to believe in God's power. Prayers of repentance eliminate the static and send our messages on through to God.

Further, just as we need God's cleansing, so we must also forgive the sins of others toward us. "Be kind and compassionate to one another, forgiving each other, just as in Christ God forgave you" (Ephesians 4:32).

Get still before God daily. Allow Him to show you areas where unforgiveness or other sins exist. Ask Him to cleanse you and reveal how to make changes in this area of your life. Once you've conquered one weak area, ask God to disclose another. Regular, careful examination of our hearts, along with a willing ear to hear what God is saying, will ensure spiritual growth. And it all happens through prayer.

5. RECOMMIT
"And lead us not into temptation; but deliver us from evil."

I realized one day that it was just as silly for me to walk out the door without going into my prayer closet as it was to walk outside without getting dressed from my clothing closet. We face incredible challenges every day, and unless God guides us through, we can fail. It's essential to pray that God will keep us from falling into Satan's snares.

God uses those temptations to draw us closer to Himself. He will do the same for our children. "Consider it pure joy, my brothers, whenever you face trials of many kinds, because you know that the testing of your faith develops perseverance. Perseverance must finish its work so that you may be mature and complete, not lacking anything" (James 1:2-4). Our children will develop virtues through the difficulties they face if God is in control. We must resist trying to rescue our kids from these hardships and pray, instead, that God will finish His work in them. We must also teach our children about pitfalls to avoid: "Watch and pray so that you will not fall into temptation. The spirit is willing, but the body is weak" (Matthew 26:41).

Above all, we must keep praying that God will deliver our children from the snares Satan lays in their paths and will work in our kids through their trials. "Blessed is the man who perseveres under trial, because when he has stood the test, he will receive the crown of life that God has promised to those who love him" (James 1:12).

Satan wants to destroy our kids. It's that simple, but it's not new. Jesus conveyed the same idea to one of His disciples: "Simon, Simon, Satan has asked to sift you as wheat." What did Jesus do? "But I have prayed for you, Simon, that your faith may not fail" (Luke 22:31-32).

Jesus knew the trials would make Simon Peter strong if they didn't destroy him in the process. So He prayed for him. Let's do the same for our children.

The one concern of the Devil is to keep Christians from praying. He fears nothing from prayerless studies, prayerless work, and prayerless religion. He laughs at our toil, mocks our wisdom, but trembles when we pray.

Samuel Chadwick

Faith

For it is by grace you have been saved, through faith—and this not from yourselves, it is the gift of God.

EPHESIANS 2:8

In John 3, we meet a Pharisee named Nicodemus. Pharisees were important leaders at that time in Israel's history, and they taught that the things a person *did* brought the greatest favor in God's eyes. Nicodemus talked to Jesus about the miracles He performed. Imagine this works-based Pharisee's surprise when Jesus responded, "No one can see the kingdom of God unless he is born again" (v. 3).

What a novel concept Jesus introduced as He went on to tell Nicodemus he had to be born of the Spirit! "For God so loved the world that he gave his one and only Son, that whoever believes in him shall not perish but have eternal life" (John 3:16). That evening became a defining moment in Nicodemus' life.

My son Clint's defining moment came on April 29, 1992, after he arrived home from kindergarten. The two of us sat at the kitchen table, eating lunch. Out of the blue, Clint asked, "Mom, how long does it take to become a Christian after you ask God into your heart?"

I had done everything I could to teach my little boy about the things of the Lord. But I knew that all my wishes, beliefs, and activities would not secure Clint's salvation. He might know the right scriptures and songs and rhetoric, but he needed a personal relationship with God. No matter how long it took, I had determined to pray for my children's personal salvation. Now, it seemed the time had come for Clint.

"Would you like to ask Jesus into your heart?" I said.

Clint nodded, and he made the most important decision of his life as he repeated the sinner's prayer:

> Dear God, to those who believe in Your name, You give the right to become Your children (see John 1:12). I want to become Your child today. I understand that Jesus, my Lord, paid the price for my sins and then rose from the dead (see Romans 10:9). Take away the sins in my heart, and help me to live the rest of my life for You.

That decision opened the door of Clint's heart for God to begin His lifelong work in him. As with Nicodemus, it was only the first step. Mom's faith had led to Clint's faith. And that faith will sustain him through all the hardships and temptations that lie ahead.

Prayer

Revere

God, You are magnificent. You told Nicodemus, "The wind blows wherever it pleases. You hear its sound, but you cannot tell where it comes from or where it is going. So it is with everyone born of the Spirit" (John 3:8). Though Your ways are mysterious, Your love and mercy are available to all. That we become Your heirs and joint heirs with Your Son, and that You dwell within us through the Holy Spirit, is more than my mind can grasp. Thank You for that gift and for extending it to everyone in my home.

Release

I know that faith means being sure of what we hope for and certain of what we do not see (see Hebrews 11:1). Help ________ to take a firm hold of that faith and trust in You even when the results can't be seen. You tell us that without faith it is impossible to please You, because anyone who comes to You must believe that You exist and that You reward those who earnestly seek You (see Hebrews 11:6). Make ________'s walk a personal one. Let ______'s prayer of salvation take a firm hold and be only the beginning of a vibrant walk with You.

Request

Never let ________ take his commitment to You lightly. Remind him that he is set apart and should live as such. Create in ________ a hunger to read Your Word and learn about You so his walk will deepen and You can show him the way he should go.

Repent

I confess that I sometimes fail to show a strong witness. I've missed opportunities to model strength, goodness, and patience. But I am so thankful that You become strong in my weakness and that Your grace is sufficient for me (see 2 Corinthians 12:9).

Recommit

Guide _________ through temptations. Be strong in her. Help me to know how to guide ________, answer her questions, and assist her toward spiritual maturity.

Things to Do

1. Tell your child the details of your own conversion to Christ.
2. Demonstrate how to sustain faith in God through troubles.
3. Discuss how to handle difficulties with your child as they occur so that when he encounters his own, he will know the process.
4. Expose your child to both high-profile and lesser-known people who profess a vibrant faith in Christ.
5. Nurture your child's spiritual growth through Bible studies, prayer, and activities at home and at church that keep the excitement alive.

Faith is not belief without proof,
but trust without reservation.

Elton Trueblood

Trouble and perplexity drive us to prayer, and prayer driveth away trouble and perplexity.

Melancthon

Commitment

Because the Sovereign Lord helps me, I will not be disgraced. Therefore have I set my face like flint, and I know I will not be put to shame.

ISAIAH 50:7

Our children live in a society that demonstrates shallow commitments. Men and women aren't called upon to die for beliefs anymore, and often don't feel compelled to *live* for anything, either. "I'll serve You, God," is easy to say during good times. But when a Christlike life becomes inconvenient or unpopular, we sometimes modify our walk with God. Our children observe these examples every day.

Daniel 3 tells the story of three men with a different kind of commitment to God: Shadrach, Meshach, and Abednego, also known as the three Hebrew children. They were among those taken into captivity by the Babylonian king Nebuchadnezzar. The king made an image of gold and forced everyone in his kingdom to worship it as a god. Anyone who refused would be burned to death in a furnace.

Nonetheless, the three young Hebrews refused to do as

the king insisted. Instead, they said, "If we are thrown into the blazing furnace, the God we serve is able to save us from it, and He will rescue us from your hand, O king. But even if He does not, we want you to know, O king, that we will not serve your gods or worship the image of gold you have set up" (Daniel 3:17-18).

The men refused to bow, and Nebuchadnezzar refused to be made to look like a fool. So he cranked up the furnace seven times hotter and threw them into the flames.

When the king looked into the furnace, he saw the men not only surviving but walking around in the fire! And a fourth man was in there with them, one who "looks like a son of the gods," Nebuchadnezzar said (Daniel 3:24-25).

The best part of all? Shadrach, Meshach, and Abednego made their choice for God *before* they knew what the result would be.

Nebuchadnezzar recognized what the Hebrew children possessed: "They trusted in [God] and defied the king's command and were willing to give up their lives rather than serve or worship any god except their own God" (Daniel 3:28). That same commitment caused them to *live* in trust as well.

Prayer

Revere

"O Lord, our Lord, how majestic is your name in all the earth! You have set your glory above the heavens. When I consider your heavens, the work of your fingers, the moon and the stars, ... what is man that you are mindful of him, the son of man that you care for him?" (Psalm 8:1, 3-4). I will worship and serve You with my life always.

Release

Blessed is _________, because his strength is in You, and he has set his heart on pilgrimage [on following You]. Because of this commitment, when he passes through the valley of tears in his life, he will make it a place of springs and pools. _________ will go "from strength to strength" (Psalm 84:5-7).

Request

Establish a faith in ___________ that's worth dying—and living—for. Help her to make her commitment to You a settled issue, a nonnegotiable fact. Surround her with circumstances and with people who will demonstrate this kind of commitment. But help her to be courageous enough to maintain her commitment even when no one applauds.

Repent

I confess that at times I've been fickle—I didn't believe just because I couldn't see the results. Help me always to be a symbol of commitment to Jesus Christ in everything I say and do.

Recommit

I pray that __________'s commitment to You and to godly principles will enable him to walk through difficult places and not give in to sin or sway his allegiance to follow the crowd. Instead, as ____________ holds on to his commitments, You will make good things grow in his life.

Things to Do

1. Reinforce old-fashioned allegiance to country. Teach your child to love and pray for the land in which she lives. Support and pray for certain missionaries (your church can provide a list) and for the countries in which they serve.
2. Teach your child that when he takes on a commitment, he sticks with it. For example, have him stay with soccer or piano lessons until the end of the season.
3. Model how to defend those you love. Moms and dads can do this every day by always presenting a united front before the children. Differences can be discussed in private.
4. Reward your child for standing firm in her beliefs, even when she stands alone.

Consider the postage stamp. Its usefulness lies in its ability to stick to one thing until it gets there.

Anonymous

Prayer is the link that connects us with God. It is the bridge that spans every gulf and bears us over every abyss of danger or of need.

A.B. Simpson

Heart

Servants, be obedient to them that are your masters according to the flesh, with fear and trembling, in singleness of your heart, as unto Christ; not with eyeservice, as menpleasers; but as the servants of Christ, doing the will of God from the heart.

EPHESIANS 6:5-6, KJV

The prophet Samuel had gone to Jesse's house in Bethlehem to do God's will—to choose the next king of Israel. He gazed upon Eliab, one of Jesse's handsome, strong, older sons, thinking surely this was the man. But God said, "Do not consider his [Eliab's] appearance or his height, for I have rejected him. The Lord does not look at the things man looks at. Man looks at the outward appearance, but the Lord looks at the heart" (1 Samuel 16:7).

Samuel examined seven of Jesse's sons this way, but none of them was the one. So Samuel asked if there were any more.

"'There is still the youngest,' Jesse answered, 'but he is

tending the sheep'" (1 Samuel 16:11).

Samuel called for David, and God said, "He is the one" (1 Samuel 16:12).

David's father and brothers looked at David and saw a lowly shepherd boy. But God had big plans for him based on what He saw inside this young man—a pure heart with undying devotion to Him. God knew that the heart is the center of a person's moral, intellectual, and spiritual life. And in Acts 13:22, God called David "a man after my own heart."

Can our sons and daughters still achieve that today? I believe they can. More than once, my children have asked to leave a movie because it contained language we cannot endorse. Recently, Clint talked to me with tears in his eyes about how he had treated another boy unkindly at school. "I've already asked God to forgive me," he said.

We can pray for God to fold His heart around theirs so that their desires, ambitions, and thoughts will be the ones He Himself has ordained for them.

Prayer

Revere

O God, what a heart You have for Your people. Your plans stand firm forever, the purposes of Your heart through all generations (see Psalm 33:11). Thank You that not only do You have a heart for me, but I can also have a heart for You. And I want that so much for myself and my family.

Release

Help ______ obey in all things those who are over him—not with eyeservice, as a manpleaser, but in singleness of heart, fearing You (see Colossians 3:22, KJV).

Request

Show ______ how to live her life, do her work, and pursue her passions—with her whole heart. Help her surrender all the parts of her heart to You and never lose her heart to anything or anyone else. Help ______ to be a person after Your heart.

Repent

How easy it is to allow my heart's allegiance to be swayed, and I have done that. I've allowed other people and plans to distract my heart from the things You would have me do and know. Forgive me for that. I surrender my whole heart all over again to You. Show me how to help ______ also renew his vows of surrender to You.

Recommit

Help ______ seek You with her whole heart and never wander from Your commands, which she has hidden in her heart (see Psalm 119:10-11). Let these commands and singleness of heart sustain ______ through the trials of her faith that are sure to come.

Things to Do

1. Always make your unswerving faith in God apparent. Let your child know that you will serve God no matter what.

2. Be sensitive to your child's tender heart. Teach him how to listen and obey God when He speaks.
3. Show your child how to guard her heart from intruders and those who could hurt her.
4. Encourage a work ethic in your home that says you work with all your heart and do a job the best you can, but you also play and rest with all your heart at appropriate times.

Set our hearts on fire with love to You, O Christ our God, that in its flame we may love You with all our heart, with all our mind, with all our soul, and with all our strength and our neighbors as ourselves, so that, keeping Your commandments, we may glorify You, the giver of all good gifts.

Eastern Orthodox Church

God will do nothing but in answer to prayer.

John Wesley

❧

Intimacy

I want to know Christ and the power of his resurrection.

PHILIPPIANS 3:10

We see her three times in Scripture—Mary of Bethany. She lived with her brother and sister, Lazarus and Martha, and Jesus visited them often.

We first read of Mary in Luke's Gospel, when she sat at Jesus' feet in their home as He taught. She forgot everything she had to do and soaked in all Jesus had to say. Martha came in and asked Jesus to tell Mary to help her with dinner preparations. But Jesus responded, "You are worried and upset about many things, but only one thing is needed. Mary has chosen what is better, and it will not be taken away from her" (Luke 10:41-42).

Mary appears next in John 11, when Lazarus became gravely ill. Martha and Mary sent for Jesus, but He didn't come right away, and Lazarus died. When Jesus finally arrived, Mary cried out to this man she adored, "If You'd been here, Lazarus wouldn't have died."

Jesus wept, followed Mary to Lazarus' grave, and raised him from the dead.

Finally, in Matthew 26 and Mark 14, we read how Mary took her most valuable possession—an alabaster jar of costly ointment—and headed toward the home of Simon the Leper, where Jesus was dining with Lazarus and others. She may well have heard on the streets of Bethany about the plot to kill Jesus, then run to get the perfume with the horror of those words burning in her heart.

Arriving at Simon's house, Mary pushed open the door and looked around the room. All the men were reclining around the table. I'm sure she hesitated as she made her way across the room in silence. Then she broke her jar and poured the ointment on Jesus' head.

"What a waste," said the men, including Judas Iscariot. "We could have fed the poor for a year with what that's worth."

"Leave her alone," said Jesus. "Why are you bothering her? She has done a beautiful thing to me. The poor you will always have with you, and you can help them any time you want. But you will not always have me.... She poured perfume on my body beforehand to prepare for my burial.... Wherever the gospel is preached throughout the world, what she has done will also be told, in memory of her" (Mark 14:4-9).

This anointing, the greatest honor a commoner could bestow on royalty, followed Jesus through the next few days in the Garden of Gethsemane, Pilate's palace, Herod's hall, and on Calvary's cross.

Mary took time to know Jesus deeply. The Bible defines this kind of knowing by the word *yada,* which means "life-giving intimacy." We find the same word in Genesis 4:1: "And Adam knew Eve his wife; and she conceived, and bare Cain" (KJV). The kind of intimacy Mary had with Jesus was not physical but led to a deep, eternal relationship. And she found it all by sitting at the feet of Jesus and adoring her Lord.

One evening when my children were about thirteen, eleven, and nine, we sat on my bed doing Bible study. Long before, I had discarded Bible storybooks and conventional curricula in favor of discussing lessons God was teaching me or issues that arose within our home. I remember talking about Joshua that night. Emotion overwhelmed me and soon overtook my children. We finished, and before Ashley walked out of the room, she said, "The stuff in the Bible is still important to us today."

When everyone else had left the room, Clint walked to the side of my bed, his thumb stuck in his Bible as a marker. "I love this," he said as he wiped his tears with the back of his other hand.

"What?" I asked.

"This," he said, raising his Bible.

Though the tears dried and we went on about our normal routines, we had each had an intimate encounter with God. We've learned that knowing God is not restricted to attending church on Sunday morning or hearing about someone else's walk with God. Instead, it can be a vibrant, daily, intimate journey with the One who knows everything about each of us.

Prayer

Revere

O Lord, one thing I ask of You, "this is what I seek: that I may dwell in the house of the Lord all the days of my life, to gaze upon the beauty of the Lord and to seek Him in his temple" (Psalm 27:4). I don't want just a mediocre existence with You; I want my family to know Your deepest secrets. For I know that You confide in those who fear You and make Your covenant known to them (see Psalm 25:14).

Release

"The people that do know their God shall be strong and do exploits" (Daniel 11:32, KJV). O God, help _______ to know You in that way. Lead him into deeper places with You.

Request

As _____ learns about the mind of Christ and becomes more like You, show her how to spread that intimacy to others. Demonstrate Your agape love for others through her. Show ______ how to find wise intimacy with others throughout her life. And then as she makes knowing You her focus, make her a strong, valiant, and radical person for You all the days of her life as she does mighty exploits in Your name.

Repent

I confess that I've put You in a box and limited Your power. I sometimes parent and even pray for ________ with my own agenda in mind. Help me to focus more on sitting at Your feet and releasing him to You. Show me how to encourage _______ to develop intimacy with You.

Recommit

As _______ faces the temptations that will come, may he be drawn ever closer to You. As in intimacy with anyone, that requires talking regularly, spending time together, and getting to know each other. I release _______ to knowing You more, being strong, and doing mighty exploits in Your name.

Things to Do

1. Sing choruses of praise and adoration every day—in the car, around the table, or during family time. Model lavishing your love on God.
2. Point out that all good things come from God (see James 1:17). When your family avoids the flu that's going around, praise God for it. When your child gets a new pair of basketball shoes, thank God for His provision. Train your child to give God credit for everything good—all because He knows and loves each of us.
3. Get your child into the habit of staying in touch with friends and relatives by writing notes or cards. This helps her learn to communicate some of the emotions she feels and draws her closer to the other person rather than staying at arm's length.
4. Build undistracted Bible reading and prayer into your family's daily schedule.

He who waits for God loses no time.

Anonymous

The prayer of the feeblest saint on earth who lives in the spirit and keeps right with God is a terror to Satan. The very powers of darkness are paralyzed by prayer.... No wonder Satan tries to keep our minds fussy in active work till we cannot think in prayer.

Oswald Chambers

Excellence

Whatever you do, do it all for the glory of God.

1 CORINTHIANS 10:31

Everyone knows the name *Moses*. He delivered the Israelites from Egyptian bondage and led them to the Promised Land. Throughout his life, he gave his best effort to everything he undertook, never doing just enough to get by.

We know the story. He was placed in the Nile River by his Hebrew mother, Jochebed, to save him from certain death at the hands of the Egyptians. The Pharaoh's daughter found him and raised him in the palace. He killed an Egyptian who beat a Hebrew laborer, then fled to Midian, where he married the priest's daughter and tended his father-in-law's flocks. There he saw a burning bush and received the call of God to free the people from slavery.

"Take off your sandals, for the place where you are standing is holy ground," God said from the flaming bush. And at the moment Moses obeyed, I believe he chose to shed everything that stood between him and God. He committed himself to excellence.

In Exodus 3–11, however, Moses made up eleven excuses for why he was not the best man to deliver Israel:

"Who am I?"

"They won't listen."

"I'm not qualified."

But God instructed Moses to begin with what he held in his hand—a staff—and do the work he was called to do (see Exodus 4:2). And Moses did. Through a long process, God used him to convince Pharaoh to free the people.

Once they crossed over into the wilderness, Moses continued to give all he had to his work. He didn't handle everything perfectly (like when he broke the stone tablets containing commandments out of anger toward the Israelites' disobedience), but he always gave his best effort.

At age 120, when Moses' "eyes were not weak nor his strength gone" (Deuteronomy 34:7), he died in Moab. And the Bible recognizes his excellence: "Since then, no prophet has risen in Israel like Moses, whom the Lord knew face to face, who did all those miraculous signs and wonders the Lord sent him to do in Egypt" (Deuteronomy 34:10-11).

When I began my job as a founding magazine editor for Focus on the Family, my boss and mentor asked me what writers I wanted to feature in the premier issue. I named those I thought would provide the best material. "But I don't want to use all my heavy hitters in one issue," I said.

"Seek excellence," he said. "Fill each issue as though it

were your last. When you need more, it will be there."

I've remembered those words in other areas of my life as well—with my children, my relationships, and my goals. And I soon learned that the well of excellence never runs dry. Then I remembered the words my father once told me: "When God's people strive for perfection, in His eyes, they're already perfect."

Moses proved that. I'm proving that. And I'm praying that my children will prove that as well, as they "take off their sandals, take up their staff," and strive for excellence in all God has called them to do.

Prayer

Revere

Your name alone, God, is excellent. Your glory is above the earth and heaven (see Psalm 148:13). "How excellent is thy loving-kindness, O God! Therefore the children of men put their trust under the shadow of thy wings" (Psalm 36:7, KJV).

Release

Your grace is sufficient for ______, for Your power is made perfect in his weakness. Therefore, ______ can boast all the more gladly about his weaknesses, so that Your power may rest on him.... For when ______ is weak, then You are strong (see 2 Corinthians 12:9-10).

Request

Be strong for ______ today. Show ______ the things that interfere with her relationship with You. Make clear the ways that You want ______ to improve her walk with You.

Repent

I confess, Lord, that I have often been content with mediocrity. Help me to pursue excellence in all areas of my life, especially in my walk with You, and so set an example for my children.

Recommit

When ______ faces temptations, help him not to give up or settle for following the letter but not the spirit of Your will. Help _____ know just what needs to be done, how to do it, and how to put that weakness behind him. Help ______ strive for excellence in all he does for Your name's sake.

Things to Do

1. Teach your child that anything worth doing is worth doing well and that a job is not done until it's done right.
2. Contrast the commitment and work habits of the average athlete and the excellent one. Showcase people who go the extra mile.
3. Help your child achieve excellence with practices or school projects.
4. Generate objectives to measure performance (e.g., chores are complete when everything has been finished and is ready for surprise inspections).

Reputations are made by searching for things that can't be done and doing them. Aim low: boring. Aim high: soaring.

United Technologies

Oh, that we would turn eye and heart from everything else and fix them upon this God who hears prayer until the magnificence of His promises and His power and His purpose of love overwhelm us.

Andrew Murray

ൽ

Teachability

Search me, O God, and know my heart; test me and know my anxious thoughts. See if there is any offensive way in me, and lead me in the way everlasting.

PSALM 139:23-24

One day as I drove my kids to school, a Christian song came on the radio. I felt overwhelmed with emotion. "Guys," I said, "listen to the words of that song."

I turned to see Clint flipping the ear of the boy riding with us. Courtney chewed her gum disinterestedly. I grew discouraged.

But then I remembered the source of my passion. I fell in love with Jesus when I found Him faithful in the tough times of my life. My children had not shared in those experiences.

In Deuteronomy 11:2-7, God warned the Israelites who had come into the Promised Land not to forget that their children hadn't seen the miracles He had done in the wilderness. They had only heard of them from their moms and dads. So the parents were instructed to recount the stories to their kids "when you sit at home and when you walk along the road, when you lie down and when you get up" (Deuteronomy 11:19).

Likewise, God reminded the people in Deuteronomy 6:10-12 that they didn't build the houses they would occupy in the Promised Land, nor did they dig the wells from which they would drink, or plant the trees whose fruit they would eat. These were all reminders of God's faithfulness. The blessings their families would enjoy didn't just magically appear; they were given by God.

Today, you and I need to remember to tell our kids about God's faithfulness in every way, praying that their hearts will remain teachable and then trusting Him to do His work in each of them.

Prayer

Revere

God, I praise You because Your way is perfect. Everything that happens in our lives passes through Your hands before it reaches us. Thank You for working all these things out for our eternal good and not just giving us what would please us today.

Release

I know You stand at the door and knock at ______'s heart. Help ______ to hear Your voice and open the door so the two of you can dine together (see Revelation 3:20).

Help ______ confess with her mouth the Lord Jesus and

believe that You raised Him from the dead so she can be saved (see Romans 10:9).

Request

Help ______ realize that You design difficulties to draw him to Yourself. Bring back to ______'s mind the things he has learned, and assist him in applying them to the hard experiences that lie ahead. Help ______ to personalize his faith in You.

Repent

I sometimes forget, Lord, that my wilderness experiences honed my true faith in You. Keep me ever learning the things You long to teach me.

Recommit

Don't let ______ ever fall into Satan's snare. Help him to stand firm through all the valleys of temptation he passes through as he learns to rely more completely on You.

Things to Do

1. Regularly discuss difficulties you encounter and what they teach you.
2. Point out people who leaned on another individual who had faith in Christ, rather than leaning on God for themselves. Show how this becomes useless during difficult times.
3. Be sensitive to the moment when your child asks to give her heart to God and subsequent times when you see God at work in her life. Celebrate and praise her teach-

ability and God's special call on her life.

4. Teach your child to measure his growth in God. For example, on January 1 every year, he can list two ways he has grown in his faith and two ways he still needs to improve. Then he can seal the envelope, open it next January 1, and evaluate how he did. He might also want to add steps toward achieving his objectives.

Should God place you on His anvil, be thankful. It means He thinks you're still worth reshaping.

Max Lucado

Men may spurn our appeals, reject our message, oppose our arguments, despise our persons—but they are helpless against our prayers.

J. Sidlow Baxter

Balance

Let your moderation be known unto all men.

PHILIPPIANS 4:5, KJV

We first meet Peter and his brother Andrew in Matthew 4:18. Jesus saw them fishing as He walked by the Sea of Galilee. They didn't know that everything would change after the day Jesus asked them to follow Him and become fishers of men. Yet they left their nets behind and went with Him.

One day, Jesus asked His disciples how others described Him. Some told Him the names they had heard, but Peter responded, "You are the Christ, the Son of the living God" (Matthew 16:16).

Peter's answer pleased Jesus, and He promised to build His church on that fact (see Matthew 16:17-18).

So Jesus groomed Peter and gave him many jobs. Yet Peter always had a tendency to get off balance.

We find an example of this in Matthew 14:23-31. Jesus had sent His disciples away in a boat while He went off to pray. A storm arose, and Jesus walked out to them on the water. After recovering from his fright, Peter wanted to try.

Peter climbed out of the boat and strolled on the water. His eyes were fixed on Jesus as he took the next step. However, he quickly grew more confident in his own abilities. But as soon as he took his eyes off Jesus, Peter sank. In an instant, he went from great faith to complete fear, and Jesus had to reach out to save him.

Then there was Gethsemane. Just before the crucifixion, Jesus prayed there with His disciples. Emotions ran high as the soldiers arrived to arrest Jesus and the disciples realized that His hours were numbered. Peter pulled his sword and struck the high priest's servant, cutting off his right ear (see John 18:10). Jesus admonished Peter to stay balanced when He said, "Peter, put your sword away."

Peter went on to deny that he knew Jesus during the hours before His trial. Then, when his lack of faith was exposed, Peter wept bitterly in repentance.

Balance comes from spending time with God each day. That causes us, like Peter, to look to Jesus for instruction. As parents, we must be sure we model godly balance for our children. They should see in us men and women who keep their eyes on God in all areas of life. They should also see us keeping the most important concerns at the top of our priority lists. Finally, they should see us praying that each of them will also find balance.

Prayer

Revere

O God, thank You for the example of balance You left for us in Your Son. He knew what imbalance would mean to His own ministry. When times were hardest, Jesus concentrated on You the most. I praise You that while You are able to do all things, through Your Son You also know what we experience as people here on earth.

Release

"Jesus grew in wisdom and stature, and in favor with God and men" (Luke 2:52). Help _____ to do the same. Show me how to teach _____ ways to grow intellectually, physically, spiritually, and socially.

Request

Thank You for the many gifts and talents You have given _____, but he also needs wisdom in how to use them. Help _____ to keep balance in his actions and reactions and what he chooses to spend his efforts on.

Repent

I confess that I sometimes live at a frantic pace and fail to model balance for _____. Help me also to grow intellectually, physically, spiritually, and socially. Show me how to respond graciously and righteously in all things.

Recommit

_____ will be tempted to participate in things that are not beneficial. It will also be easy for her to spread herself too thin. Provide wisdom in these areas, and make _____ an example of godly balance.

Things to Do

1. Maintain schedules and routines in your home whenever possible.
2. Model setting healthy boundaries and saying no to unnecessary involvement.
3. Know what you can do, and don't do any more than that. Make time to relax or do something you enjoy each day.
4. Help your child prioritize the activities he chooses as well as the ways he spends his time.

The main thing is to keep the main thing the main thing.

Anonymous

Prayer is essentially man standing before his God in wonder, awe, and humility; man, made in the image of God, responding to his maker.

George Appleton

Service

The greatest among you will be your servant. For whoever exalts himself will be humbled, and whoever humbles himself will be exalted.

MATTHEW 23:11-12

James and John traveled with Jesus as His disciples. Their parents wanted the best life had for them. So one day their mother knelt down reverently before Jesus and said, "Grant that one of these two sons of mine may sit at your right and the other at your left in your kingdom" (Matthew 20:20-21).

Jesus responded by explaining the difference between the world's way of thinking and His. "You know that the rulers of the Gentiles lord it over them," He began, "and their high officials exercise authority over them" (v. 25).

Examples of what He said must have flooded into the minds of all who listened. Their world applauded status, wealth, and lordship. Of course they would want to be among the great men who exercised authority over others.

But Jesus continued, "Not so with you. Instead, whoever wants to become great among you ..."

That's us! That's what I want for my boys, James and John's mother probably thought. But her thinking quickly turned upside down as Jesus finished His message.

"... must be your servant, and whoever wants to be first must be your slave—just as the Son of Man did not come to be served, but to serve, and to give his life as a ransom for many" (Matthew 20:26-28).

One winter day, I pulled into a gas station to fill up my tank. My son generally takes care of this job, but he couldn't remove the stuck cap. I tried and failed as well.

Then two men in their late twenties drove up in an old, dirty car. "Evening, ma'am," one said.

"Hello," I said. "Would you be able to help us get our gas cap off?"

One man started pumping their gas while the other helped us. When the man at the other pump finished, he came to my car and tried his hand at the gas cap while his friend went inside to pay. With the help of a screwdriver from his car, he finally popped the lid off.

By that time, the man from inside had returned. "You look cold," he said. "Let me pump that for you."

We chatted while he filled my tank. I said "thank you" to both men and followed the one man inside, where he finished his business and I wrote my check. When I handed the cashier my check, he said, "It's already taken care of. That man paid for your gas."

I turned to thank the man, unsure of what had just happened, but he was gone. His car and his friend were gone, too.

As my family and I drove away that cold January night, I thought about how our lives had been touched by two people with servants' hearts—in word and in deed. I wondered if God was just at work in their lives or if their moms and dads had taken the time to teach and pray that they be givers rather than takers. Perhaps they taught them not to *grab* for the best, but instead to *give* their best—in all circumstances.

Prayer

Revere

O God, creator of heaven and earth, how truly marvelous You are. And yet with all Your splendor and majesty and omnipotence, You chose to send Your Son to earth to be a servant to us all. He rolled up His sleeves and washed others' feet and taught His disciples to do the same: "Now that you know these things, you will be blessed if you do them" (John 13:17).

Release

God, You tell me that if ________ will faithfully obey the commands You give him—to love You and serve You with all his heart and soul—You will send rain on his land in its season, and he will eat and be satisfied (see Deuteronomy 11:13-15). I pray with all my heart that ________ will, indeed, love and serve you all the days of his life.

Request

Create opportunities for ____ to serve others. Help ____ recognize those opportunities and be willing to serve in them.

Repent

I acknowledge that I don't always model a servant's heart. Sometimes I get so busy that my focus narrows, and I forget to reach out to others. Help me to see and change that kind of attitude every day, and teach me how to help create serving opportunities for _____.

Recommit

There will be times when ____ has to choose between serving others and indulging herself. Give _____ strength to make the right choice, even when no one around her does. Make her sensitive to how pleased You are with those decisions, and remind her that Your Son came to serve, not to be served.

Things to Do

1. Involve your family in regular service together (soup kitchens, missions sponsorship, your local church).
2. Teach your child to give of his money as God has blessed him, and allow him to watch you do the same. This practice comes from the Bible, in verses such as Malachi 3:10.
3. Point out others who serve.
4. Read and memorize Bible verses on service and servants, such as the ones found in this devotional. Refer to them

often, and tie them in with events that occur in your child's life.

We can hide from God in our service to Him and fill our minds with learning about Him without our hearts being captured by Him.

Oswald Chambers

There is no gift like prayer, for in prayer we find a Father who welcomes us, who listens and always understands, peace in the perspective of eternity ... strength to hold on and wait for God to work, a haven in His presence, a safe place to keep those we love.

Unknown

Silence

When you are on your beds, search your hearts and be silent.

PSALM 4:4

Elijah needed to learn how to be silent before God, even with noise all around him. In 1 Kings 19, he ran from Queen Jezebel and King Ahab, who were trying to kill him. He fled into the wilderness and sat down under a broom tree, where he prayed for God to take his life. What happened?

He slept (v. 5).

He obeyed the Lord's command to eat good foods: "All at once an angel touched him and said, 'Get up and eat ... for the journey is too much for you'" (vv. 5, 7).

He grew spiritually (v. 11).

He found a friend (v. 19).

But even with all these good things, Elijah needed more. He needed to learn how to be silent. "Then a great and powerful wind tore the mountains apart and shattered the rocks before the Lord, but the Lord was not in the wind. After the wind there was an earthquake, but the Lord was not in the earthquake. After the earthquake came a fire, but the Lord was not in the fire" (vv. 11-12).

Where was God? "And after the fire came a gentle whisper" (v. 12).

God does not oppose the good things that keep us busy. He does not reside in the stresses of our lives, however, though He upholds and guides us through them when we ask. Instead, He lives in the quiet places where, like Elijah, when we finally stop our activities, we can hear what He has to say.

Frederick Buechner, in his book *Now and Then,* advised wisely, "Listen to your life. See it for the fathomless mystery that it is. In the boredom and pain of it, no less than in the excitement and gladness! Touch. Taste. Smell your way to the holy and hidden heart of it because in the last analysis, all moments are key moments and life itself is grace."

One day when my children were young, I told them that the day belonged to us to spend as we pleased. I told them to choose the activity.

"Let's just stay home," Ashley said.

"Yeah!" agreed the other two.

So we spent the day at home and enjoyed the quietness and one another's company.

I'm praying that such experiences will become practice for adult times when each of my kids will need wisdom to know when to speak and do and go, and when to be silent.

"In repentance and rest is your salvation, in quietness and trust is your strength" (Isaiah 30:15).

Prayer

Revere

How great You are, God. And how wonderful it is to come before You. I find You in the quiet of my bed or wherever that personal prayer place is each day. How beautiful it is to hear You speak quietly to the issues of my life through Your Holy Spirit.

Release

Help _____ to be still and know that You are God (see Psalm 46:10). Teach _____ to be still before You and wait patiently for You (see Psalm 37:7).

Request

Help _____ to never get too busy or schedule his day too full to be silent before You. Teach him to enjoy silence and solitude. Give _____ a taste for quietness and meditation in his heart, even at an early age.

Repent

I confess that I jam too much into our lives. Much is what I consider service to You and for my children. But some of the greatest gifts I can give ____ are a gentle and quiet spirit (see 1 Peter 3:4) and a peaceful, quiet, and holy life (see 1 Timothy 2:2).

Recommit

Help ____ not to fall into the trap of overinvolvement.

Show ____ how to prioritize, choose wisely, and simplify her life. Give her discernment for the times when things get too chaotic.

Things to Do

1. Reserve Sundays and evenings after a certain time for rest.
2. Model how to choose activities wisely and not overextend yourself.
3. Allow your child to see you reserve daily quiet time.
4. Don't overcommit either your child or yourself.
5. Keep extraneous noises (TV or radio) to a minimum in your home.

How do we keep the world from shaping us into its own image? In solitude, I get rid of my scaffolding. Silence makes us pilgrims. Silence guards the fire within us. Silence teaches us to speak words ... that form the floors, walls, and ceiling of our existence.

Henri Nouwen

Our prayers lay the track down on which God's power can come. Like a mighty locomotive, His power is irresistible, but it cannot reach us without rails.

Watchman Nee

Gratitude

Be joyful always; pray continually; give thanks in all circumstances.

1 THESSALONIANS 5:16-18

Job suffered boils all over his body and lost vocation, home, cattle, seven sons, and three daughters. He cried out, "Even today my complaint is bitter; His hand is heavy in spite of my groaning" (Job 23:2). But Job prayed anyway: "He knows the way that I take; when He has tested me, I will come forth as gold" (Job 23:10).

David walked through deep valleys and looked for God there: "I remembered you, O God, and I groaned; I mused, and my spirit grew faint" (Psalm 77:3). But then David recalled God's goodness and gave Him praise: "Your ways, O God, are holy. What god is so great as our God? You are the God who performs miracles; you display your power among the peoples. With your mighty arm you redeemed your people" (Psalm 77:13-15).

Jeremiah blamed God for walling him in, weighing him down, keeping him in darkness, barring his way, making his paths crooked, mangling him, and leaving him without hope. "I remember my affliction and my wandering, the bitterness and the gall. I well remember them, and my soul is downcast within me" (Lamentations 3:19-20). But then he acknowledged the great God he served: "Yet this I call to mind and therefore I have hope: Because of the Lord's great love we are not consumed, for his compassions never fail. They are new every morning; great is your faithfulness" (Lamentations 3:21-23).

What caused Job, David, and Jeremiah to look up amid such harrowing circumstances? I believe they each possessed a grateful heart. They cherished the blessings God had already given and knew He would continue to provide. That gave them cause for rejoicing.

It's not always easy to remember all we have for which to be thankful. One morning found me discouraged about problems I faced with one of my children. I put in the back of my mind the other times God had taken care of us, and I worried about what could happen. I bit my lip and fought back tears as I drove.

Suddenly, Clint spoke from the seat beside me and snapped me back from my reverie. "Just look where we live, Mom," he said. He pointed to the majestic Front Range of the Rocky Mountains toward which we were driving. "God is so good to us."

"He sure is," I said.

May I learn to keep the same perspective and pray that Clint continues to count his blessings instead of his misfortunes.

Prayer

Revere

My heart will sing to You and not be silent. O Lord my God, I will give You thanks forever (see Psalm 30:12).

Release

Whatever _____ does, whether in word or deed, help him to do it all in the name of the Lord Jesus, giving thanks to You, the Father (see Colossians 3:17).

Help me to teach _____ to enter into Your gates with thanksgiving and into Your courts with praise, giving thanks to You always (see Psalm 100:4).

Request

Just as Job, David, and Jeremiah did, help _____ to remember Your glory and faithfulness even in trying circumstances. Use these difficulties to build _____'s faith.

Repent

I confess that I've missed opportunities to teach my child to be grateful. And forgive me for the times I have failed to thank You myself.

Recommit

Please don't let _____ get into the habit of complaining. Instead, help her to count her blessings at all times and see Your glory everywhere.

Things to Do

1. Give thanks for all things in your children's hearing (meals, money, friends, sunshine). Resist complaining.

2. During quiet times, take one evening a week to offer round-robin thanks to God without asking Him to do anything else for you.
3. Share from your bounty with the less fortunate—not just a onetime offering, but giving generously and regularly to those in need.
4. Make thanksgiving a regular and essential part of all family prayers (e.g., before bed, meals, or trips).

Thou hast given so much to me. Give me one thing more—a grateful heart. Not thankful when it pleaseth me, as if Thy blessing had spare days, but such a heart whose pulse may be Thy praise.

George Herbert

What marvelous power there is in prayer!
What untold miracles it works in this world!
What untold benefits does it secure to those who pray!

E. M. Bounds

Patience

The end of a matter is better than its beginning, and patience is better than pride.

ECCLESIASTES 7:8

Be joyful in hope, patient in affliction, faithful in prayer.

ROMANS 12:12

Mankind has learned to speed things up in many ways: cooking with microwaves, communicating through e-mail, working via computers. But we've never figured out how to wait quickly. We all go through times when life puts us on hold and we can do nothing about it but wait. And wait. And wait. Does God prevent His people from having such experiences? No; instead, He knows that the more desperate the wait, the more willing the ear will be to hear what God has to teach the person.

The Israelites experienced a seventy-year wait in Babylon. They didn't want to be there and didn't know how long they'd have to stay. But God told Jeremiah to write them a letter and explain what to do while they waited: build houses and settle down, plant gardens and eat, produce families, seek peace and prosperity (see Jeremiah 29:4-9). Though the Israelites would rather have had Jeremiah deliver them *from* the wait, at least they had a letter with God's instructions for what to do *through* the wait. So what did the Israelites do? They obeyed God, and they waited until He delivered them from their captivity.

On another occasion, Hezekiah, king of Judah, received a letter from Sennacherib, king of Assyria, who threatened to annihilate God's people. Hezekiah read the letter, then went to the temple and spread it out before God. "O Lord," he prayed, "listen to all the words Sennacherib has sent to insult the living God" (Isaiah 37:17). He continued to pray, and then he waited. He waited until the angel of the Lord put to death 185,000 Assyrian soldiers (see Isaiah 37:36).

Many years ago, my family and I started a tradition of making lists on January 1 of the things God had done for us in the preceding year and the things we trusted Him to do in the year ahead. We wrote this information on a sheet of paper, sealed it in an envelope, filed it away, and then waited for God to meet our needs. One year later, we opened the letter, rejoiced at the ways in which God had moved, and submitted new requests. Many needs transferred from year to year, and we still wait for answers to some.

What we're doing with that tangible reminder is giving everything to God and trusting Him to do His work, in His time. That requires patience and trust. Habakkuk 2:2-3 says, "Write down the revelation and make it plain on tablets so that a herald may run with it. For the revelation awaits an appointed time; it speaks of the end and will not prove false. Though it linger, wait for it; it will certainly come and will not delay."

Because we can't always solve our problems by microwaving provisions, e-mailing answers, or working with sophisticated computers, we wait. We have the choice of waiting with or without patience. But if we truly trust God as did the Israelites, Hezekiah, and Habakkuk, we must wait patiently as He does His work. Let's teach our kids to do the same.

Prayer

Revere

"Wait for the Lord; be strong and take heart and wait for the Lord" (Psalm 27:14). God, You know all things. Thank You that You have my family's whole life in Your hands. I surrender us all to Your sovereignty.

Release

No one whose hope is in You will ever be put to shame. Guide ______ in Your truth and teach him, for you are ______'s Savior, and his hope is in You all day long. May integrity and uprightness protect him (see Psalm 25:3, 5, 21). I know that if _____ waits on You, he will grow strong and mount up like an eagle (see Isaiah 40:31). Let it be so.

Request

Give ______ the wisdom to rejoice in her sufferings so You

will have an opportunity to produce perseverance, character, and hope. As ______ works through problems with school, siblings, parents, or illness, let her know that You maintain hidden contact with her life as You did with Joseph when he was sold into slavery in Egypt. Help _____ resist the tendency to grow impatient with Your timing.

Repent

I know Your timing is impeccable, God, though I sometimes wish You'd hurry up. Forgive me. I surrender my desire to do things my own way and to stop waiting on You. Help me guide ______ in doing the same.

Recommit

As _____ grows and encounters more temptations, let him always remember in his heart that no one who waits on You will ever be sorry. Let him recall the things You've done for him before and be courageous enough to stand firm when he doesn't see the answer forthcoming. Let _____ never compromise during his waits.

Things to Do

1. Tell about your own experiences when it seemed God did not care and how He answered in the end.
2. List past prayers answered.
3. Demonstrate how to pray for something, then how to wait for God's answer.
4. Bake, sew, or build something together that requires a lot

of time for individual steps. Show how essential it is to take time to do each step well.

Most people give up just when they're about to achieve success. They quit on the one-yard line. They give up at the last minute of the game one foot from a winning touchdown.

H. Ross Perot

God shapes the world by prayer. The more praying there is in the world, the better the world will be, the mightier the forces against evil.

E.M. Bounds

Sensitivity

And Moses said, "Here I am."

EXODUS 3:4

And [Isaiah] said, "Here am I. Send me!"

ISAIAH 6:8

Since the beginning of time, God has extended His call to His people in unique ways. His call is not just for a special few, either: "Many are invited, but few are chosen" (Matthew 22:14). The call of God is for everyone who will hear Him *when* He calls.

Isaiah overheard God saying, "Whom shall I send?" (Isaiah 6:8).

Abraham was living with his barren wife in Haran when God asked him to take his possessions and go to a land He would show him (see Genesis 12:1).

Moses was tending flocks on the far side of the desert for his father-in-law when God called him to free the Israelites from Egyptian bondage (see Exodus 3:4, 10).

Elisha was plowing in the fields with twelve yoke of oxen

when God called him to succeed Elijah (see 1 Kings 19:19).

David was herding sheep as the second youngest of Jesse's sons when Samuel came to Jesse's house and appointed David to be the second king of Israel (see 1 Samuel 16:11-13).

Gideon was threshing wheat in a wine press to hide it from the Midianites when he heard God's call (see Judges 6:11-12).

God calls many different kinds of people to do many different kinds of work: Abraham was rich, but Gideon was poor. Moses was old, while David was barely a teen. God also uses various means to get people's attention: an angel for Gideon, a burning bush for Moses, a prophet for David. He met David on a hillside, Gideon by the wine press, Moses in the desert. He called some to be kings, others to be prophets, and still others to be writers.

One day Clint asked me, "Mommy, what does it sound like when Jesus talks to you?"

We discussed it, and then he continued, "The other night, I was trying to go to sleep, and I heard someone call my name. I looked up and didn't see anyone. But I knew it was Jesus 'cause He was talking to here"—he patted his chest—"He wasn't talking to my ears."

"What did Jesus say to you?" I asked him.

"He said, 'I love you, Clint,'" Clint replied.

Clint is growing more sensitive to Christ. He'll need to keep his ears tuned to the voice of God, and he'll need me to pray that he does.

Prayer

Revere

"What is man that you are mindful of him, the son of man that you care for him?" (Hebrews 2:6). You know each of us intimately and call us by name. How I love You, Lord!

Release

I'm amazed that You, God, chose _____ and appointed him to bear fruit. And You have promised that whatever he asks in Your name, You will give (see John 15:16). Help _____ to realize the absolute wonder of those rights. Let him know how intimately You know and understand him and that You have a special work for him to do.

Request

Keep _____ in the center of Your will. Don't let her make choices that will mess up the plans You have for her. Instead, let her learn to hear Your voice and feel Your leading.

Repent

At times, I try to interfere with Your work in _____'s life. Let me know where to step in and where to back off. Do Your complete work in _____.

Recommit

Don't let _____ fall into any temptation that will cause him to forfeit Your blessings. Don't let him go in directions that will cause him to take Your second best rather than Your very best. And always, always, give him a sensitive ear for what You're saying to him.

Things to Do

1. Expose your child to people and places that confirm the things you teach.
2. Let your child meet Christians who are happy and fulfilled while living a godly life.
3. Help your child explore the things in which she's interested. They may be the beginnings of God's call in her life.
4. Train your child to listen to the voice of God. Be sure he understands God is there for him, to protect as well as to guide.

The chosen ones are those who have come to a relationship with Jesus and had their dispositions altered and ears unstopped to hear the call, "Who will go for us?" God does not plead.

Oswald Chambers

Expect resistance, but pray for miracles.

Corrie ten Boom

Fairness

My brothers, as believers in our glorious Lord Jesus Christ, don't show favoritism.

JAMES 2:1

The message of Christ shattered walls of prejudice and exclusion. He became an advocate for everyone.

For children. The disciples rebuked people when they brought their children for Jesus to touch. But Jesus said, "Let the little children come to me, and do not hinder them, for the kingdom of heaven belongs to such as these" (Matthew 19:14).

For different ethnic groups. The Samaritan woman said to Jesus, "You are a Jew and I am a Samaritan woman. How can you ask me for a drink?" (John 4:9). But Jesus turned tradition on its head when He moved to more important matters and told her about the living waters He had to give her.

For the downcast and needy. A Canaanite woman with a demon-possessed daughter pursued Jesus. The disciples urged Him to send her away. But Jesus healed her daughter (see Matthew 15:28). And in John 7:24, He said, "Stop judging by mere appearances, and make a right judgment."

For sinners. Jesus ate dinner at Levi's house with sinners and tax collectors. The Pharisees questioned the wisdom of this (see Mark 2:16). Jesus answered, "It is not the healthy who need a doctor, but the sick. I have not come to call the righteous, but sinners" (Mark 2:17).

One day I received a call from Courtney's third-grade teacher. "I just wanted to tell you," she said, "what a neat girl you have. We took a field trip today, and Courtney cared for our Down syndrome student, Sara. Courtney left her group of friends and tended to Sara's needs all day long."

Isn't that what Jesus would have done? And if we're in Him, shouldn't we be about similar good works? Shouldn't we shed the mentality that we're more entitled than the poor, the homosexual, the murderer? The salvation message is for everyone. The end of the Bible reads, "The Spirit and the bride say, 'Come!' And let him who hears say, 'Come!' Whoever is thirsty, let him come; and whoever wishes, let him take the free gift of the water of life" (Revelation 22:17).

Prayer

Revere

You, God, do not show favoritism but accept people from every nation who fear You and do what is right (see Acts 10:34-35). I praise You for that, because somewhere in Your acceptance, You chose me to be Your child. With You there is no difference between Jew and Gentile. You're the same Lord to all and richly bless all who call on You (see Romans 10:12).

Release

Give _____ the courage to speak up for those who can't speak for themselves and for the rights of all who are destitute. Help _____ to stand firm, judge fairly, and defend the rights of the poor and needy (see Proverbs 31:8-9).

Request

Show _____ how to share your love with everyone, all the time. Help _____ not to see himself as better than anyone else, but only as blessed to have received the gift of salvation. Let _____ not be in bondage to racism or bias but to shine Your love in the hearts of everyone.

Repent

I confess that at times I feel a sense of entitlement. You don't owe me anything, yet You gave me Your Son freely. Except for Your blessings, I would be among the poorest and most unlovely. Your grace made the difference. Let me never forget that.

Recommit

_____ will be tempted to blame You when things are going badly. She could start to believe You owe her blessings. She might sometimes treat others as she would never want to be treated herself. Help her to resist those temptations and lavishly share the gifts of love and grace with others as You have given them to her.

Things to Do

1. Expose your child, whenever possible, to other cultures, socioeconomic groups, and races.
2. Have people from other countries and different ways of life come to your home for a meal.
3. Share news with your child from the mission field. Support a needy child.
4. Teach your child to give love gifts, above his regular offerings, to the less fortunate.

Fairness needs love as the seed in the cold earth needs the nurture of the warming sun. But love needs fairness as the flowing river needs its firm clay banks. Love may be the heavenly vision, but fairness is the guiding light.

Lewis Smedes

Prayer is not a vending machine which spits out the appropriate reward. It is a call to a loving God to relate to us.

Philip Yancey and Tim Stafford

Responsibility

"Well done, good and faithful servant! You have been faithful with a few things; I will put you in charge of many things. Come and share your master's happiness!"

MATTHEW 25:21

From the beginning, men and women have been blaming others for their own poor choices. When God asked Adam if he had eaten from the forbidden tree, Adam replied, "The woman you put here with me—she gave me some fruit from the tree, and I ate it" (Genesis 3:12).

Adam passed on this failure to take responsibility for his own actions to his sons. When God questioned Cain after he killed Abel, Cain asked, "Am I my brother's keeper?" (Genesis 4:9).

Failure to take responsibility for oneself is also epidemic in our time. W.T. Purkiser says, "One of the great sources of moral and political breakdown in our day is the reluctance of ordinary people to accept responsibility."

In contrast, Thomas Jefferson once wrote,

- Never put off till tomorrow what you can do today.
- Never trouble another for what you can do yourself.
- Never spend your money before you have it.
- Nothing is troublesome that we do willingly.

One day recently, someone told me my daughter was doing something that did not reflect well on her Christian walk. The news disturbed me greatly. I wanted to march up to her and challenge her with what she had done. But instead, I marched before God and said, "Please show me how to handle this."

By the next morning, I knew. As we drove to school, I told her what had been reported to me. I didn't ask for a defense, as I had wanted to do earlier. Instead I said, "You are now fully responsible to God. You can always hide something you do from me, but never from God. He sees all, and He does not tolerate compromise. The worst part of compromise isn't the bad things you do; it's the good things you miss out on."

Only a few weeks have passed since that talk with Courtney. I've had no more reports of the behavior I heard about earlier. I *have* had numerous reports about the Christian leadership she exhibits—volunteering to discuss her faith and stepping in to help someone in need.

I pray that all these experiences help Courtney to know her responsibility before God for her own actions. And I pray she will never say "He made me do it" but will instead be answerable for the kind of person she becomes.

Prayer

Revere

"The heavens are yours, and yours also the earth; you founded the world and all that is in it" (Psalm 89:11). And because I'm Your child, You have set me in a spacious place (see Psalm 31:8). I have nothing to lose and everything to win with You on my side.

Release

Help ______ to test his own actions and take pride in himself without comparing himself to others. Help him to carry his own load without blaming others for his actions (see Galatians 6:5).

Request

God, thank You for helping us to be better moms and dads. If left on our own, we'd all be sunk. You love my child , _____, even more than I do. Please help her take charge of herself in both her thoughts and her conduct.

Repent

I admit I've missed opportunities to pray for my child and to model my own responsibility to You. Help me to hold myself accountable to others, and help me always to realize the consequences of my choices. Then help me to pass on this information to my children.

Recommit

Don't let _____ ever fall into the world's error of failing to take responsibility for oneself. Let him know that when he became Yours, all became new. Help _____ to be confident that You will guide and protect him through every trial, temptation, and test.

Things to Do

1. Be sure your child is responsible for household chores, homework, extracurricular activities, after-school jobs, and volunteer work. Make responsibilities clear, consistent, and commensurate with the child's developmental stage.
2. Help your child choose short-term social, physical, and spiritual goals; such as "plan a party for a few friends," or "memorize a favorite psalm." Choose some long-term goals as well: write to grandparents twice a month, learn to play a musical instrument in the coming year, read the Bible every night before bed.
3. At the beginning of the year, have each member of the family list the ways he has done better in the social and physical areas (as well as the spiritual, which we talked about earlier). Then have each person write down how he can do better in the next year. After discussing them, put the lists in envelopes and seal until next January, when you repeat the process.

A crowd in its very concept is untruth. It renders the individual completely impenitent and irresponsible, or at least weakens his sense of responsibility by reducing it to a fraction.

Søren Kierkegaard

Holy Spirit, think through me till Your ideas are my ideas.

Amy Carmichael

&

Wisdom

My son, pay attention to my wisdom, listen well to my words of insight, that you may maintain discretion and your lips may preserve knowledge.

PROVERBS 5:1-2

The Lord brought me forth ... before His deeds of old; I was appointed from eternity; from the beginning, before the world began.

When there were no oceans, I was given birth, when there were no springs abounding with water; before the mountains were settled in place, before the hills, I was given birth, before He made the earth or its fields or any of the dust of the world.

I was there when He set the heavens in place, when He marked out the horizon on the face of the deep, when He established the clouds above and fixed securely the fountains of the deep, when He gave the sea its boundary so the waters would not overstep His command, and when He marked out the foundations of the earth.

Then I was the craftsman at His side.

I was filled with delight day after day, rejoicing always in His presence, rejoicing in His whole world and delighting in mankind.

Now then, my sons, listen to me; blessed are those who keep my ways.

Listen to my instruction and be wise; do not ignore it.

Blessed is the man who listens to me, watching daily at my doors, waiting at my doorway.

For whoever finds me finds life and receives favor from the Lord. But whoever fails to find me harms himself; all who hate me love death.

PROVERBS 8:22-36

No words can add to Solomon's definition of wisdom. She was the beginning of everything, the craftsman at God's side. And today, she is the one who helps our children to apply knowledge. She is the one who will sort out life and cause our kids to think with God's mind.

Courtney went to visit an unsaved friend. When she returned, I asked if she'd had the opportunity to witness.

"Yes," she said, "but not in words. I just thought my actions would speak louder than my words."

Wisdom had talked to Courtney. If God needed wisdom in the beginning, how much more do our kids need her now?

Prayer

Revere

God, thank You for the wisdom You give Your people. You left us Your Word as a lamp to our feet and a light to our paths (see Psalm 119:105). This light will illuminate our way through all of life, and we'll never have to stumble aimlessly in the dark.

Release

"The fear of the Lord is the beginning of knowledge, but fools despise wisdom and discipline" (Proverbs 1:7). Place a love deep inside _____ for Your wisdom and discipline. Let _____ always be thankful instead of resentful of the boundaries and guidelines a godly life imposes.

Request

Help _____ get wisdom and understanding. Don't let him forget Your words or swerve from them (see Proverbs 4:5). Hide them in _____'s heart so he won't sin against You.

Repent

I confess that I often fail to seek wisdom. It's there for the knowing if I ask and read Your Word. Help me to cultivate that wisdom every day so I can be more and more like You.

Recommit

Grant _____ wisdom to avoid the bad and surround herself with people and things that are good for her. Give her the wisdom to put to work, in productive and healthy ways, the knowledge she has gained. As _____ begins laying her own foundations for life, let her always remember that "by wisdom a house is built, and through understanding it is established; through knowledge its rooms are filled with rare and beautiful treasures" (Proverbs 24:3-4).

Things to Do

1. Play a game while you drive or during some informal time together. Name certain situations, and have the

children identify them as knowledge or wisdom. For example, multiplication facts are knowledge; not shoving your beliefs down someone else's throat is wisdom. Discuss how knowledge grows into wisdom.

2. Set aside a special time for thirty-one days to read the book of Proverbs, one chapter per day. Do it in a comfortable setting where you can serve snacks. Allow discussion to follow the reading.

Wisdom grows when knowledge is lived.

Sidney B. Simon

Prayer constantly enlarges our horizon and our person. It draws us out of the narrow limits with which our habits, our past, and our whole personage confine us.

Paul Tournier

Peace

"Peace I leave with you; my peace I give you. I do not give to you as the world gives. Do not let your hearts be troubled and do not be afraid."

JOHN 14:27

In 2 Kings 4, we read how the prophet Elisha arrived in the town of Shunem and stayed with a wealthy couple who had prepared him a small room in their home. Because of their kindness, Elisha prayed for God to bless them with a son, and He did. The son grew and worked with his father in the fields, but one day he suffered sunstroke. The father carried his son into the house. The mother held her son until he died, then laid him on the prophet's bed and had her husband saddle a donkey for her.

She took off in search of Elisha and found him at Mount Carmel. When Elisha saw her coming, he said to his servant, "Look! There's the Shunammite! Run to meet her and ask her, 'Are you all right? Is your husband all right? Is your child all right?'" (2 Kings 4:25-26).

"All is well," she said. "Oh, by the way, my son is dead. Could you come and raise him back to life?"

Elisha and his servant followed the woman back to Shunem. The prophet stretched out over the dead body of the woman's son and restored his life.

What gave that woman peace in the midst of her difficulty? She knew deep inside that God controlled all things.

When I was a child, my large family encountered incredible difficulties—illness, financial problems, and issues with the church Dad pastored. I would hear my parents talk about the challenges. Still, I could go to bed at night and sleep peacefully because I knew my mom and dad would take care of everything.

A few weeks ago, I spent time praying about several issues that concerned me and my family. I took out my well-marked Bible and found several scriptures God had given me for circumstances in the past. I ran my finger across each of them and reviewed them, much as I would old love letters. I needed to remind myself how much Someone loved me, just how sufficient His grace was for me, and how much He was in charge of all the details of my life.

Then I rolled over in my bed to go to sleep. Like the Shunammite woman, I knew all was well.

Prayer

Revere

"You are my refuge and strength, an ever-present help in trouble. Therefore, I will not fear, through the earth give way and the mountains fall into the heart of the sea, though its waters roar and foam and the mountains quake with their surging. There is a river whose streams make glad the city of God, the holy place where the Most High dwells" (Psalm 46:1-4).

Release

You will keep _________ in perfect peace because his mind is steadfast and he trusts in you (see Isaiah 26:3).

Request

Please let _________ know You are there for her no matter what she faces. Talk to her in quiet moments. Give her direction for decisions she faces. And always give her the peaceful assurance that all is well as long as she is in Christ.

Repent

Sometimes I let myself grow worried, and I wonder if You know about a certain difficulty I face. Forgive me. I know You know. You have always been faithful and will be forever.

Recommit

Let _________ realize the importance of communing with You and letting You fill his spirit with Your peace. Don't permit hardship and temptation to scare the peace out of him.

Things to Do

1. Read stories of great heroes of the faith who remained calm when things were going badly.

2. Memorize scriptures on peace. I found a note under Ashley's pillow once where she'd written out a promise of peace for when she's afraid.
3. When your family is fearful or troubled about something, sing. Help your children cultivate the habit of doing this.

One of the titles by which Jesus is known is Prince of Peace, and he used the word himself in what seemed at first glance to be two radically contradictory utterances ... Matthew 10:34 ... and John 14:27. The contradiction is resolved when you realize that for Jesus, peace seems to have meant not the absence of struggle, but the presence of love.

Frederick Buechner

Solitude and silence can never be separated from the call to unceasing prayer.

Henri Nouwen

Encouragement

A man finds joy in giving an apt reply—and how good is a timely word!

PROVERBS 15:23

Joseph lost many things unfairly. His jealous brothers stole his robe, threw him into a hole, and then sold him into slavery (see Genesis 37). When he ended up in Egypt, he found himself working for one of Pharaoh's officials, Potiphar. Once more, Joseph was mistreated when his master's wife grabbed his robe and said he had tried to seduce her (see Genesis 39).

So there Joseph sat in a filthy, damp prison. After twelve years, two of Pharaoh's officials—the chief cupbearer and the chief baker—also landed in jail. Though Joseph had spent more than a decade unfairly confined in that awful place, he said to the men, "Why are your faces so sad today?" (v. 7).

Even in the midst of his own problems, he was willing to encourage others.

I wish I had that ability mastered better. Once I stood at a department-store counter, writing a check for merchandise

I had purchased. A little girl stood in front of me with her mother. My preoccupation with the errands I needed to run was interrupted when the little girl asked me, "Are you mad?"

Thankfully, that doesn't always happen. My children and I took a trip back to Indiana. Though we had lots to do and many people to see, we went with my sister and nieces to visit my ninety-year-old uncle. He talked of his ailments, and he said as he pointed a shaking finger toward his lip, "This cancer will probably spread to other places in my body."

"Can you talk to God about these things, Uncle Conley?" I asked.

"Oh, no," he said. "Me and the Lord ain't friends. I done too much. He cain't forgive me."

Later, I had the privilege of leading him in the sinner's prayer as he *did* experience God's forgiveness through Jesus Christ. Several months later, Uncle Conley died.

What a joy it was to lay aside my own agenda and discomforts and minister to someone else! Joseph also learned this lesson. Two years after he encouraged the cupbearer and baker, Pharaoh brought him out of prison and made him second in command in the land of Egypt. This time he didn't have his robe taken away but a new robe placed on him (see Genesis 41:42).

Prayer

Revere

"Praise be to You, the Father of compassion and the God of all comfort, who comforts me in my troubles so that I can comfort others with that same comfort" (2 Corinthians 1:3-4).

Release

You tell us in Isaiah 58:6 to pray and fast "to loose the chains of injustice and untie the cords of the yoke, to set the oppressed free and break every yoke."

Request

Help _______ always to realize he should be about Your business—even when he faces problems of his own. Let encouraging words and kind acts be part of his everyday interaction with other people. Let him always offer to others the hope of Christ that You offer him.

Repent

I confess that at times I've been so caught up in my own issues that I have missed opportunities to encourage others. Help me to model being a source of encouragement for _________.

Recommit

Let _________ take her temptations and turn them into opportunities to witness for You and encourage others in the faith. Don't let _________ get lost in her own concerns.

Things to Do

1. Train your child always to look at the positive side of life.
2. Teach your child that if everything belongs to God anyway, why worry? Show how to share this good news with others.
3. Hold each other accountable to say kind, encouraging words to each other.
4. Cultivate the habit of sending notes of encouragement to people in need.

Do you know someone who has:
a song waiting to be sung?
some art waiting to be hung?
a piece waiting to be played?
a scene waiting to be staged?
a tale waiting to be told?
a book waiting to be sold?
a rhyme waiting to be read?
a speech waiting to be said?
If you do, don't let them die with the music still in them.

Florence Littauer

Unceasing prayer needs to be sought at all costs, even when the flesh is itchy, the world alluring, and the demons noisy.

Henri Nouwen

&

Purity

Don't let anyone look down on you because you are young, but set an example for the believers in speech, in life, in love, in faith, and in purity.

1 TIMOTHY 4:12

The issue of sexual sin is as old as mankind itself. People tend to chafe at all the biblical commands concerning sexual conduct. But God created us, so He knows what's best for us. He didn't create the laws for legalistic reasons or to give us a shadow to live under. He gave us laws to provide the best lives possible.

Proverbs 7:6-23 illustrates this explanation of God's sexual laws:

At the window of my house I looked out through the lattice. I saw among the simple, I noticed among the young men, a youth who lacked judgment. He was going down the street near her corner, walking along in the direction of her house at twilight, as the day was fading, as the dark of night set in. Then out came a woman to meet him, dressed like a prostitute and with crafty intent. (She is loud and defiant, her feet never stay at home; now in the street, now in the squares, at every corner she lurks.) She took hold of him and kissed him and with a brazen face she said: "I have fellowship offerings at home; today I fulfilled my vows. So I came out to meet you; I looked for you and have found you! I have covered my bed with colored linens from Egypt. I have perfumed my bed with myrrh, aloes and cinnamon. Come, let's drink deep of love till morning; let's enjoy ourselves with love! My husband is not at home; he has gone on a long journey. He took his purse filled with money and will not be home till full moon." With persuasive words she led him astray; she seduced him with her smooth talk. All at once he followed her like an ox going to the slaughter, like a deer stepping into a noose till an arrow pierces his liver, like a bird darting into a snare, little knowing it will cost him his life.

What principles can we extrapolate from that young man's experience to teach to our own children?

- Wisdom and understanding will help you conquer sexual sin (v. 4).
- Don't go where you shouldn't go, see what you shouldn't see, or talk or listen to those you shouldn't (v. 8).
- Sin looks good (v. 5).
- Sin is crafty (v. 10).
- Sin doesn't give up (vv. 11-12, 15).
- Sin attacks when you're most susceptible to its advances (v. 13).
- Sin says it's OK (v. 14) and everybody's doing it (vv. 19-20), but the end result of sin is death (v. 23).

With my own children, I try to subtly reinforce the truth in these scriptures at unexpected times: modeling them myself, exposing my kids to people who have messed up their lives with sexual sin, and pointing out godly young men and women who maintain strong stands for purity.

Recently, Courtney has been demonstrating her understanding of the truth in this Proverbs passage at unexpected times. During a ride home one night, for example, I heard her and one of her Christian friends in the back of the car talking about sexual abstinence. A few weeks later, as we rode to a soccer game, she talked of desiring to find a female professional athlete to mentor her and show her how to balance her walk with Christ, her sport, and her academics. We sat in front of a sandwich shop in Denver while Courtney went to God with this request.

God's laws were given for our good. Courtney knows this, and she's applying His principles to her life.

Prayer

Revere

God, You sent Your Son to live as a man on this earth. He experienced every temptation mankind faces, yet He was without sin. I praise You for Your love and Your holiness.

Release

I pray for purity in ______ —not just sexual purity, but also the kind that begins deep inside. For when sin occurs, it reflects a deeper heart problem. But blessed is _____ because of his pure heart, for he will see God (see Matthew 5:8).

Request

Help ______ realize that she can't play with fire and not be burned. Help her understand that she can't go to wrong places or associate with wrong people or listen to wrong counsel and not get off track. We see people everywhere who are unhappy and in distress because of failures to control tempers, appetites, passions, and impulses. Let ______ always distinguish the truth from the lie, even when the voices around her are telling her wrong is right. Help her to recognize Satan's subtle attempts to destroy her. But help her also to realize she can do all things through Christ who gives her strength (see Philippians 4:13).

Repent

Sometimes I don't demonstrate a pure heart. My words reflect other motives. Help me to model that same deep purity I want for my child.

Recommit

______ will face temptations as he grows up that I never knew existed when I was his age. But Your Word says that where there's much sin, there's much more grace (see Romans 5:20). Let grace be with ______ everywhere he goes.

Things to Do

1. Stress sexual, emotional, and spiritual purity to your child while she's young. Involve her in a youth group, sports, and volunteer work.
2. Give your child alternatives. When he's older, provide

ideas for staying pure on dates—things to do and things not to do.

3. Introduce your child to the "True Love Waits" campaign, and give her a purity ring and/or a "What Would Jesus Do?" bracelet. The important thing to let your child know is that we do—and don't do—certain things because we want above all else to honor Jesus.

Our Lord often calls His church His bride. Like a bride of beauty and purity in no other color than white, all Christians represent that they are pure, "spiritual" virgins awaiting the joys and intimacies of heavenly marriage with their Groom.

Chuck Swindoll

The literal translation of the words "pray always" is "come to rest."

Henri Nouwen

Generosity

"Give, and it will be given to you. A good measure, pressed down, shaken together and running over, will be poured into your lap. For with the measure you use, it will be measured to you."

LUKE 6:38

An expert in the law stood before Jesus and asked about the route to eternal life and the command to love his neighbor as himself. "And who is my neighbor?" he asked Jesus (Luke 10:29).

Jesus answered with a story about a man going down from Jerusalem to Jericho who had fallen into robbers' hands. They stripped him, beat him, and left him half dead. A priest came along, but when he saw the beaten man, he walked by on the other side of the road. Then a Levite arrived at the scene, but he, too, avoided the injured man.

Next came a Samaritan, who saw the man and took pity on him. He bandaged thc man, loaded him on his donkey, and took him to an inn where he could receive proper care.

The next day, the Samaritan paid the innkeeper and promised to cover the injured man's additional expenses until he recovered.

"Which of these three do you think was a neighbor to the man who fell into the hands of robbers?" Jesus asked.

The expert in the law replied, "The one who had mercy on him."

Jesus told him, "Go and do likewise" (Luke 10:36-37).

Go and do likewise. The Samaritan man gave of his time, money, and talents—from his heart—to help a complete stranger. That pleased Jesus, because when God's people minister to others' needs, all become neighbors.

My children and I have developed a custom of volunteering at inner-city soup kitchens. This desire began in me when I was in my early twenties and working at my first teaching job. I went to a nursing home a few doors from my apartment and volunteered on Thursday evenings to read and do crafts with the women there.

This wasn't easy for me: My evenings could have been spent on something more entertaining, the craft supplies cost money I couldn't spare, and the smell and atmosphere of the home depressed me. I sometimes dragged myself to my Thursday night commitment. I always floated home, however. I'll never forget the nimbleness and talent of the older women who could no longer communicate or the universal appeal of the songs we sang. Those Thursday evenings made a difference in the women's lives, in my life, and now in the lives of my kids as I pass the experience on to them.

One recent winter night, thirteen-year-old Courtney encouraged me to go and pick up twelve-year-old Tony. We know his family, and he had called after he got locked out of his house. I had a horrendous schedule to keep, and I knew his mother would be home in less than an hour. But Courtney's encouragement caused me to realize that we needed to be a safe place for that boy to call when he got in trouble.

Luke 14:13-14 says that when we give to those in need, our repayment comes "at the resurrection of the righteous," not in what we get back at the moment. But I get a little piece of my reward every time my children display generosity.

I grabbed my jacket and headed out the door to pick up Tony, thankful that both of us are learning the importance of giving.

Prayer

Revere

You give so abundantly to Your people, God. You loved us so much that You gave Your only Son to die on the cross. That's generosity!

Release

Help ______ to cast his bread upon the waters so that after many days he will find it again (see Ecclesiastes 11:1). "One man gives freely, yet gains even more; another withholds unduly, but comes to poverty. A generous man will prosper; he who refreshes others will himself be refreshed"

(Proverbs 11:24-25). Let _____ give happily of his time, resources, and talents to others, because You love a cheerful giver (see 2 Corinthians 9:7).

Request

Once again, God, generosity begins with Mom and Dad. Help ______ to remember that You have given to us so we can give to others. Help her to find joy in being a giver rather than a taker and to recognize the need for generosity with her time, money, and talents.

Repent

I confess that I'm not generous with all I have. I sometimes resent a person calling and taking my time. I often wonder why the beggar can't work like everyone else. And I fail to show compassion for the person who is down on her luck. Help me to have a heart for Your people and give to them as You would. But also help me to be wise about how I spend my time and energy.

Recommit

We live in a "gimme, gimme" society where everyone asks, "What's in it for me?" Help __________ to rise above this mentality and give to others with a happy heart.

Things to Do

1. Teach your child to give his money regularly to God's work, as well as his time, such as in Bible study before bed. Let him see you do the same.

2. Help your child focus her talents for God's use. For example, singing or playing a musical instrument can be done at church or in some ministry outreach.
3. At Christmastime, allow your child to share some of his own bounty with the less fortunate. Let him have a part in deciding what you will do.

Generosity is not merely a trait which pleases God. It is a practice which releases us from bondage to self, and also to things.

Albert E. Day

For this is our Lord's will—that our prayer and our trust should be alike, large.

Julian of Norwich

Compassion

Love each other as I have loved you. Greater love has no one than this, that he lay down his life for his friends.

JOHN 15:12-13

There just wasn't enough of Jesus to go around. He resisted Satan's temptations, called His disciples, and taught the Beatitudes and how to pray. He went on to heal the leper, the centurion's servant, Peter's mother-in-law, the demon-possessed man, the paralytic, and the blind and the mute. He must have been exhausted as He went into all the villages.

Instead of letting His exhaustion and overwork dull His heart for the people, however, "when he saw the crowds, he had compassion on them, because they were harassed and helpless, like sheep without a shepherd" (Matthew 9:36). That's when He told His disciples, "The harvest is plentiful but the workers are few. Ask the Lord of the harvest, therefore, to send out workers into his harvest field" (vv. 37-38).

So what is the harvest field? And who are the workers?

Once when Ashley was nine months old, we came home to our freshly cut Indiana field of hay and heard that a severe storm was moving in. Knowing the rain would ruin the fodder, my husband got on the phone and tried to find help for the work. We called this one and that one, but everyone was busy or otherwise unavailable.

Finally, my husband pulled out the tractor and wagon, and I drove with Ashley between my legs while her dad pulled bales onto the wagon. We closed the doors on the barn, with two wagons-full inside, just before the rains began to fall.

I wonder about the chances you and I have missed to work in the fields for God because we, too, were busy or unavailable. When have we exchanged compassion for preoccupation in our own lives?

Let's be wise about nurturing our children's seeds of compassion. Let's model laying aside our own agenda for God's plan to be fulfilled. Let's regularly expose our children to opportunities to recognize and then minister to those in need—on the mission field, at the soup kitchen, or in the classroom. If we get too exhausted or overworked for this to occur, something needs to give. We need to assess what we're doing right and what we can do better—or what we should surrender. Compassion accompanies demonstration, not explanation. And remember that opportunities to practice compassion happen at times and in ways we least expect.

Prayer

Revere

Thank You, God, for the compassion You show for Your people through Your Son, Jesus Christ. That compassion reached down and loved and saved me. Help me to pass it on.

Release

Help _____ to be devoted to others in brotherly love and to honor other people, even above himself (see Romans 12:10). Show him how to do that in a wise and healthy way.

Request

It's easy to get caught up in our own lives and not see the hurting people around us. Keep _____'s heart tender toward You and Your people. Let _____ always extend a hand of love in Jesus' name.

Repent

Sometimes I fear my heart grows calloused to those in need. Forgive me, and open my eyes to what Jesus saw in hurting people. Then show me how to help.

Recommit

The tendency in _____, as in all of us, is to be so preoccupied with her own needs and struggles that she fails to notice those of others. Keep a tender and compassionate heart in _____, and show her how to remove the blinders from her vision.

Things to Do

1. As a family, volunteer at a soup kitchen or other location where you can serve those in need.
2. Give money to the poor, either locally or on the mission field.
3. *Never* allow your child to make fun of other people.
4. Expose your child to others with physical or mental handicaps.

Compassion is the sometimes fatal capacity for feeling what it's like to live inside somebody else's skin. It is the knowledge that there can never really be any peace and joy for me until there is peace and joy finally for you, too.

Frederick Buechner

Oh, that we would turn eye and heart from everything else and fix them upon this God who hears prayer.

Andrew Murray

Initiative

I can do everything through him who gives me strength.

PHILIPPIANS 4:13

Hebrews 11 is the faith hall of fame. It honors people from the Old Testament who showed creativity, initiative, and just plain guts based on the promise that the Messiah *would* come. They dared to live their lives differently from those around them.

What made Noah gutsy enough to build something called an ark to withstand something called a flood when it had never even rained before? Why did a wealthy man like Abraham leave everything behind, uproot his family, and proceed toward something unknown in a direction he was not sure of? How could Abraham be willing to offer his long-awaited son, Isaac, as a sacrifice before the Lord? Where did Moses find the courage to regard disgrace for the sake of God as of greater value than the treasures of Egypt (see Hebrews 11:7-26)?

All these people were still living by this creative faith when they died. They had not received the promise—who was Jesus. They only saw it from afar. They were so convinced of the promise, however, that they considered themselves strangers on this earth, passing through on their way to a better place. All of them left behind the things in their past because "if they had been thinking of the country they had left, they would have had opportunity to return. Instead, they were longing for a better country—a heavenly one" (Hebrews 11:15-16). This gave them creative license and initiative to do and be and dream anything instead of being like everyone else and settling for mediocrity and the status quo. Daring to be different—that's what their initiative required.

I ask Courtney, when she returns from a camp or an overnighter with a friend, about ways she found to witness. Clint prays every night, "God, I'd like to play basketball in the NBA someday, if it's OK with You. But I'll always serve You no matter what else I ever do."

We don't know where life will take our kids, but when we choose to follow Jesus without reservation, the means become the end until we get to our ultimate reward in heaven.

Let's help prepare our children to be among those gutsy, creative, modern-day heroes who dare to be the people God has called them to be. We should teach them about the difficult road their decisions will lead them down and how to defend their faith.

God's heroes are being made every day—those who dare to be different and set apart, creatively doing the work He has placed before them. I pray that some of those heroes are coming from my home and yours.

Prayer

Revere

The first words of the Bible tell us that You *created* the heavens and the earth. You pulled out all the stops. You used creativity and initiative as You put mankind and our beautiful world together. How wonderful is Your work, Lord!

Release

Show _____ that whatever his hand finds to do, he should do it with all his might, no matter what's been done before him, because "in the grave there's neither working nor planning nor knowledge nor wisdom" (Ecclesiastes 9:10).

Request

Help _____ to be among those who dare to show initiative in their work for You. Help her choose to be different. Set her eyes on the city out there whose builder and maker is God. Help her focus her eyes on eternal things and think creative, eternal thoughts.

Repent

Sometimes I have wanted to fit _____ into a mold when, according to Psalm 139, You threw away his mold once he was created. Who am I to decide what You do with his life? Give me the courage to let go and the wisdom to lead _____. Help me to demonstrate initiative and creativity myself.

Recommit

Don't let _____ get swallowed up by the average. Help her to dream bigger dreams, the ones You have placed inside her.

Things to Do

1. Read about Bible characters as well as modern men and women who dared to be different and set apart for God.
2. Encourage your child's creativity in every area. Help him explore new fields of interest.
3. Help your child think of ways she can put her talents to work for God.
4. Be sure your child knows that God's people are usually not in the majority and often stand completely alone. Point out those Christians who rise above the rest, completely sold out to Him.

Thou seest but a part of the picture, but I see the design in its completion. Thou canst not know what is in My mind and what I am creating with the materials of thy life.... I make no idle strokes. What I do is never haphazard. I am never merely mixing colors out of casual curiosity. My every move is one of vital creativity, and every stroke is part of the whole. Never be dismayed by apparent incongruity. Never be alarmed by a sudden dash of color seemingly out of context. Say only to thy questioning heart, "It is the Infinite wielding His brush; surely He doeth all things well." And in all that He doeth with a free hand, without interference, He can stand back and view the work and say, "It is good."

Frances J. Roberts

Great revivals always begin in the hearts of a few men and women whom God arouses by His Spirit to believe in Him as a living God.... Upon their heart He lays a burden from which no rest can be found except in persistent crying unto God.

R.A. Torrey

Passion

Whatever you do, work at it with all your heart, as working for the Lord, not for men.

COLOSSIANS 3:23

Having grown up as one of eight children, I vividly remember our family vacations. Once we took off to sightsee and visit my uncle in Arizona for two months. But we were barely out of our home state when tempers began to flare. We ran low on money, slept in the car, and fried eggs on a grill by a roadside picnic table. My dad drove longer hours to get us where we were going more quickly, which made him more tired, and things got worse. Excitement for the trip soon turned into exhaustion, dread, and a desperate desire to return home.

Many start off their Christian journeys in the same way—with a bang. They wake up and jump out of bed, passionately awaiting whatever comes next. They attack every challenge with gusto, enthusiasm, and every skill they have. But long hours, endless miles, crowded conditions, breakdowns, and searing heat (spiritually speaking) can quickly take the excitement away, especially when they don't pace themselves properly. David and Joshua learned this lesson and wrote about it.

David began one of his writings with "I love you, O Lord, my strength" (Psalm 18:1). Then he told why God was his rock, fortress, deliverer, shield, horn of salvation, and stronghold. Through brushes with death and destruction, David cried out for help, and he wrote, "From his temple he heard my voice; my cry came before him, into his ears" (Psalm 18:6).

David went on to talk more of God's goodness, and he ended with, "I will sing praises to your name. He ... shows unfailing kindness to his anointed, to David and his descendants forever" (Psalm 18:49-50).

How did David run a kingdom without burning out, much less keep a song in his heart? We know he struggled with losing his passion as much as anyone. In Psalm 51:12, he asked God to give him back his original joy—his beginning excitement for the journey. Like everyone else, he had to pace and protect himself, and he had to make sure he was on good terms with God. That meant stopping, pulling back from activity, reassessing the situation, confessing his sins, and replanning his strategy.

Joshua found it necessary to do the same. With his leadership, the Israelites swept into the Promised Land, conquering their enemies. But throughout the book of Joshua, we read that he rose early to pray in order to keep his bearings. He even stopped all activity in Joshua 12, and everyone sat around naming the thirty-one victories God had already accomplished through them. No conquests. No strategizing. No pilfering. Families probably brought picnic lunches as they pulled themselves back together and remembered the important things that would sustain them in the battles that lay ahead.

For *neither* David nor Joshua was life perfect; they faced ongoing challenges and difficulties. *Both* David and Joshua found that they had to pace themselves if they were to maintain their passion for God. They certainly had reason to rejoice, even in the midst of hardship. Battle number thirty-two is no sweat when one remembers what God did in the previous thirty-one. But they couldn't do it if they were physically depleted. Working with all your heart, which we read about above in Colossians 3:23, also means stopping, resting, laughing, and prioritizing with all your heart in order to maintain stamina and passion.

When I was a teenager, I attended a Bible college one summer with another girl, Laura. We hung out in the evenings with a friend, Geneva, who lived in the area. Geneva wasn't a Christian and didn't want to hear about God, but as the three of us laughed a lot together, Laura and I couldn't stop talking and singing about God's goodness.

At the end of the summer, Geneva trusted in Jesus as her Savior. "What was it that changed your mind?" I asked, thinking it was some dynamic words of wisdom I had imparted.

"It was your joy and passion for life. I wanted that, too," she said.

Prayer

Revere

I don't have to read past the first two chapters in Genesis to see the passion with which You approached creating the world, Lord. Yet You also rested on the seventh day. Help me to learn from Your example.

Release

"Never be lacking in zeal, but keep your spiritual fervor, serving the Lord. Be joyful in hope, patient in affliction, faithful in prayer. Share with God's people who are in need. Practice hospitality" (Romans 12:11-13). You want passion from _____, but show him from his early days how to do this properly and with much wisdom. Because no matter what _____ does with his life, he should do it all for the glory of God (1 Corinthians 10:31). And that takes wisdom as well as passion.

Request

"Therefore, my dear brothers, stand firm. Let nothing move you. Always give yourselves fully to the work of the Lord, because you know that your labor in the Lord is not in vain" (1 Corinthians 15:58). Help _____ to realize that eyes are always watching her. Help her to believe that You are in charge and able to do all things for her. Show _____ how to run the best race by pacing herself.

Repent

I confess that I tend to overwork and overextend myself. Help me to be a better model in this area.

Recommit

I pray that _____ will first of all commit to the race and with passion will accept the baton and run with all his strength. But I also pray for wisdom. Show him how to renew and preserve that strength for the steps ahead. Finally, let all _____ does be to Your glory and honor, and may his passion be ever evident for the work to which You call him.

Things to Do

1. Help your child explore her passions. Participate with her. Listen carefully. Plan well.
2. Build rest and relaxation into your family's regular schedule. Show your child how to do this.
3. Praise your child for jobs well done. Visibly extend more privileges as your child shows excellence in other areas.

The ones Christ chose siphoned off the pain of guilt, the embarrassment of failure, and the confusion of mixed motives and goals. Then He repainted the big picture of the original call to servanthood so that Peter was able to function again. What was the result? He restored Peter's spiritual passion. And that's what needs to happen to all of us with regularity.

Gordon MacDonald

If we consider how many dangers impend every moment, fear itself will teach us that no time ought to be without prayer.

John Calvin

Gentleness

A gentle answer turns away wrath, but a harsh word stirs up anger.

PROVERBS 15:1

In John 4, we read how Jesus came to a town in Samaria called Sychar. He sat down by a well to rest. When a Samaritan woman arrived to draw water, Jesus asked for a drink. He knew the woman inside and out. She had had five husbands and presently lived with another man. That day, Jesus gently presented to the thirsty woman a new way of life through Him. Then, leaving her water jar—and her old life—behind, the woman went back to tell others about Him.

When I read that story, I remember as a child visiting my aunt and uncle one time in southern Arizona. A stray cat had wandered onto their property, and I decided to tame it. I put out all kinds of food, but when the cat drew near, I jumped up from my hiding place and chased it until it was out of sight. I never did succeed in making that cat my summer pet.

Apparently I didn't learn my lesson well. Recently, a young woman contacted me about the need to straighten out her life. She had left her husband and had given birth to a little girl by another man who refused to marry her. I jumped right in, wanting her to undo the last fifteen years in a day. That approach scared her off.

I prayed for wisdom. Now I hope I'm lending a helping hand more the way Jesus would. He offered eternal hope through gentle love. That's what made the woman leave her old life behind—nothing else.

Prayer

Revere

Gently You woo us to Yourself, Lord. You don't bang us over the head for poor judgments, but You kindly lead by Your Word as well as Your example. What more do I need?

Release

Lord, help Your servant ______ not to quarrel or be resentful with others. Instead, help him be kind and gentle to those who oppose him while You lead them to repentance and the knowledge of Your truth (see 2 Timothy 2:24-25). "The wisdom that comes from heaven is first of all pure; then peace-loving, considerate, submissive, full of mercy and good fruit, impartial and sincere. Peacemakers who sow in peace raise a harvest of righteousness" (James 3:17-18).

Request

God, help me demonstrate gentleness in every way I interact with my children. Let them see You working in my life through how I parent them as well as how I witness to others.

Repent
I confess that I sometimes fail to love the unlovely and am impatient with those who struggle. Show me how to be gentle with all people.

Recommit
_____ will have people treat her wrongly. I pray that You will give her a wise and gentle answer to turn away their anger. Lead her victoriously through the trials she will face.

Things to Do

1. Get a pet. Demonstrate how being gentle is the quickest way to develop trust.
2. Describe a time when you got to witness for Christ as you respected the boundaries of others, leading them to ask about your beliefs.
3. Study together one of the Gospels (Matthew, Mark, Luke, or John). Make a list of all the ways Jesus reached souls with His gentleness.

Take time to be tender. Fragile and delicate are the feelings of most who seek our help. They need to sense we are there because we care, not just because it's our job.

Charles Swindoll

Another angel, who had a golden censer, came and stood at the altar. He was given much incense to offer, with the prayers of all the saints.... The smoke of the incense, together with the prayers of the saints, went up before God from the angel's hand.

REVELATION 8:3-4

Perseverance

Perseverance must finish its work so that you may be mature and complete, not lacking anything.

JAMES 1:4

I've always liked to run. In every race, all the runners start out of the chutes similarly, but then the contest becomes an individual thing. Each race offers a clearly marked course, though the route becomes apparent only as we move ahead. I'm not sure where I'm going, but I know that if I just keep putting one foot in front of the other, I'll eventually reach my goal.

One especially memorable race took place on a rainy Saturday morning in June. Determination marked my hobbled steps as I made my way to pick up my number. A throbbing sprained ankle and nausea from my pregnancy were not enough to keep me home.

The gun sounded. My ankle throbbed some more. Rain

plastered my hair against my cheeks and eyes. Gnawing pain in my tummy constantly reminded me I would be a mother in a few months.

None of those things held me back. I followed the course one aching, nauseated, drenched step at a time. At the top of a hill just past the halfway point, I caught a glimpse of the sun breaking through the clouds. I couldn't help but notice the early summer smells of redwoods and other plants.

The finish line ribbon warmed my heart as I felt it fall to my side. I had finished 157th out of 175, but I had finished—in spite of the obstacles.

Hebrews 12:1 tells us to throw aside everything that hinders us and persevere in the race. Though we can't *see* the finish line, we know we'll successfully reach it if we keep running with God.

One evening I took Courtney to the emergency room after she broke the growth plate in her ankle during a soccer game. She received bad news from the doctor: "No track, basketball, or soccer for six weeks—maybe longer."

Silently she hobbled to the car. On the way home she said, "Mom, I can't believe how quickly something can be gone that I counted on so much. The only thing we can count on and keep working toward is God."

Small words, big truth. Our kids each have an individual race to run that is different from our own. Let's not hold them back or shield them from injury or confine them to a race that's not what God designed. Instead, let's help them lay aside every weight that hinders them. And then let's help them hear what God is teaching them.

Prayer

Revere

"I will praise you, O LORD, with all my heart; I will tell of all your wonders. I will be glad and rejoice in you" (Psalm 9:1-2).

Release

Let ______ not become weary in doing good, for at the proper time he will reap a harvest if he does not give up (see Galatians 6:9). Don't let ______ ever give up or lay down his Christian armor.

Request

"He who stands firm to the end will be saved" (Matthew 24:13). Help ______ to discover the course You have laid out for her. Show her how to set aside everything that might be a hindrance. Assist ______ in seeing something bigger and better out there than the average person sees, and help her to keep Your finish line always in sight.

Repent

At times, I've grown weary and been tempted to turn back. Always remind me that there's nothing to go back to.

Recommit

I pray that ______ will have perseverance for the long haul. Help ______ to be faithful to the end.

Things to Do

1. Encourage your child to dream big.
2. Acquaint your child, through reading or real-life experi-

ences, with those who have overcome great obstacles to reach a goal.

3. Model perseverance by overcoming obstacles and staying in the race of life yourself.

Never give in, never give in, never, never, never, never—in nothing, great or small, large or petty—never give in except in conviction of honor and good sense.

Winston Churchill

More things are wrought by prayer than this world dreams of.
Alfred Lord Tennyson

Friendliness

> Greater love has no one than this, that he lay down his life for his friends. You are my friends if you do what I command. I no longer call you servants.... Instead, I have called you friends.
>
> JOHN 15:13-15

Abraham Lincoln once said, "The better part of one's life consists of his friendships." Jesus demonstrated that fact. Though He was God, He showed human emotions. In the beginning of His ministry, He proved He could do His work alone. He preached the stirring Sermon on the Mount and taught about murder, adultery, fasting, and prayer. He healed. Then He chose friends to walk with Him. He called them the twelve apostles. Those men walked, talked, ate, and learned with Jesus. But three of them—Peter, James, and John—became His closest friends.

Jesus went to the Garden of Gethsemane to talk to His Father the night before His crucifixion. He was afraid and sad and even prayed, "My Father, if it is possible, may this cup be taken from me" (Matthew 26:39). For this most crucial, defining moment in His life, Jesus included His friends: "He took Peter and the two sons of Zebedee along with him" (v. 37).

Jesus needed friends just like you and I.

Clint came home from school one day in sixth grade after having an argument with his best friend, Steve. I encouraged Clint to look at bigger issues than the ones that had made him upset with his friend, but I couldn't get through to him. "I didn't do anything," he insisted.

Two weeks went by. Then one afternoon he had the carpool drop him off at my office. About the same time, I received a call from Steve's dad. Clint had made fun of Steve at school. The other parent and I agreed to meet and talk at a fast-food restaurant.

We went inside, and two twelve-year-old boys began to cry. They talked about the ways they had been hurt—about hard, cruel, unthinking statements and their impact. Both boys said they wanted to remain friends, and both understood the areas where they had failed.

The boys have been friends ever since, though neither will ever forget the hurtful incidents. A few weeks later, however, one of their classmates was killed in a car accident. I lay down beside Clint before he went to bed that night, and he talked about the girl who had died. "I just saw her this afternoon," he said. "I didn't say goodbye."

Clint cried, then he added, "And I was thinking, what if I had not said I was sorry to Steve and something like this happened to him? I would never forgive myself."

We can help our kids both to choose and to be good, godly friends. (Chuck Swindoll says of a boy who plays in the backyard mud with white gloves on, "The gloves always get muddy; the mud never gets 'glovey.'")

Like Jesus, we all need friends. But also like Jesus, we need to find individuals who can enhance our walk with the Father. Jesus chose His companions carefully, and so should we.

Prayer

Revere

Thank You, God, for being a friend who sticks closer than a brother (see Proverbs 18:24). Other friends have let me down, but You never have. While we walk on earth, however, we need special friends. Thank You for allowing me both to be a friend and to enjoy them myself. And thank You for the criteria You give us in Your Word for who those friends should be.

Release

"A man of many companions may come to ruin" (Proverbs 18:24). Guide ______ in his selection of friends, beginning with his relationship with You. Block all relationships that are not in Your will.

Request

Jesus, You did not limit Your friendships to the twelve apostles. Instead, You extended that privilege to all of us: "You are my friends if you do what I command. I no longer call you servants, because a servant does not know his master's business. Instead, I have called you friends, for everything that I learned from my Father I have made known to you" (John 15:14-15). Let _____ understand how awesome that fact is—that as long as she keeps Your commands, she is Your friend and You whisper the secrets of the universe in her ear.

Repent
I admit that sometimes I don't obey Your commands. I never want to lose my intimacy with You, so help me to live uprightly.

Recommit
Help _____ to understand that his greatest friend of all is sticking closer than a brother and that You know and understand everything about him. Let _____ always be accountable to You for the actions You always see, and help him learn to consult You about everything in his life.

Things to Do

1. Be sure your child sees your friendships in operation. Demonstrate what makes them work as well as what makes them fail (e.g., staying in touch versus not staying in touch; keeping secrets versus telling everything you know).
2. Help your child develop the habit of writing or calling friends.
3. Teach your child this rhyme: "Make new friends but keep the old/One is silver and the other gold."

A relationship is a living thing. It needs and benefits from the same attention to detail that an artist lavishes on his art.

David Viscott

If you pray to refresh your soul, then you will feel the burning arrows of the enemy against you. However, you should not give up prayer on that account, but you should stand firm. Because that is the way to our home above, and he who gives up prayer because of it is like a man who runs away from battle.

Giles of Assisi

Confidence

So do not throw away your confidence; it will be richly rewarded.

HEBREWS 10:35

Jesse had asked his son David to take grain and bread to his brothers on the battlefield. When David arrived, he heard a giant from Gath named Goliath screaming threats against the Israelites. David asked, "Who is this uncircumcised Philistine that he should defy the armies of the living God?" (1 Samuel 17:26).

From the beginning, David recognized that no matter how big the enemy, that foe had pitted himself against God by opposing the Israelites. David's confidence in God convinced him he had nothing to lose, so he offered to fight Goliath. When King Saul heard of this, he sent for David. David told how God had proven Himself faithful to him in the fields while he guarded his sheep against the lion and the bear. "The Lord who delivered me from the paw of the lion and the paw of the bear will deliver me from the hand of this Philistine," he told the king (v. 37).

David knew that he plus God equaled everything he would ever need to defeat his enemies.

When our children were young, they looked up to us as being able to do everything, know everything, and protect them from everything. As they grew older, their eyes were opened to our shortcomings. At the same time, we hope we have shown them that when we're weak, we become strong in Christ (see 2 Corinthians 12:10). And with enough practice watching the family go through difficulties and come out OK through God, they can apply this same truth in their own lives.

Once, eleven-year-old Ashley visited some people who didn't believe in God. They talked about things that contradicted her beliefs. Upset, she went off by herself and prayed, asking God what to do. She opened her Bible, which she had brought along, to these verses: "There will be terrible times in the last days. People will be ... having a form of godliness but denying its power.... But as for you, continue in what you have learned and have become convinced of, because you know those from whom you learned it, and how from infancy you have known the holy Scriptures, which are able to make you wise for salvation through faith in Christ Jesus" (2 Timothy 3:1-2, 5, 14-15).

What more could I ask for? Ashley was learning confidence in God for herself, and that confidence can take her through anything she will ever face. Like David, she can stand boldly against any Goliath and slay him. As long as she remains in God, she can be confident that the small sling she holds in her hand will be powerful enough to defeat the enemy through the might of the great God she serves.

Prayer

Revere

Thank You, Lord, that Your grace is sufficient for me and my family (see 2 Corinthians 12:9). I don't have to be strong or smart enough to slay my giants. You can do it through me. I have found You faithful while working in the fields, facing my own lions and bears. I learned there that You would always be with me. Thank You for that.

Release

Help _____ to remember he can do everything through You as You give him strength (see Philippians 4:13), but he can do nothing without You. Let _____ never grow confident in his own abilities, but certain of Yours.

Request

If _____'s heart does not condemn her, she has confidence before You and can receive anything she asks from You—when she obeys Your commands and does what pleases You (see 1 John 3:21-22).

Repent

God, I have often trembled at the giant that stood before me. Help me more and more to trust in Your strength, not mine, and to demonstrate this confidence to my children.

Recommit

Help _____ to apply confidence in You to his schoolwork, relationships, difficulties, and temptations. Help him to find You faithful to himself, even when I'm not around.

Things to Do

1. Let your child see your confidence in God. When money is short, remind her that God will supply all your needs. When illness comes, remind her that Jesus' stripes purchased our healing. Then let her see you rest in that confidence.
2. Expose your child to people who have received answers to prayer.
3. During family devotions, keep track of prayers answered as well as those still before God. Let your child get accustomed to taking everything to God and watching as He answers.

What doth hinder us?... What but the presence of a veil in our hearts?... It is woven of the fine threads of the self-life, the hyphenated sins of the human spirit. They are not something we do, they are something we are.... Self-righteousness, self-pity, self-confidence, self-sufficiency, self-admiration, and a host of others like them.

A. W. Tozer

The ceremony of lifting up our hands in prayer is designed to remind us that we are far removed from God, unless our thoughts rise upward; as it is said in the psalm, "Unto thee, O Lord, do I lift up my soul."

John Calvin

Honesty

I have no greater joy than to hear that my children are walking in the truth.

3 JOHN 4

In Acts 5, we see a portrait of dishonesty. Ananias and Sapphira sold some property and withheld part of the proceeds. They offered the rest to the Lord, laying it at the apostles' feet and saying it was the full amount of the sale. But Peter said, "Ananias, how is it that Satan has so filled your heart that you have lied to the Holy Spirit and have kept for yourself some of the money you received for the land?... What made you think of doing such a thing? You have not lied to men but to God" (Acts 5:3-4).

Ananias heard Peter's words and fell over dead.

Soon his wife, Sapphira, appeared. She didn't know what had occurred in her absence. Peter asked her, "Is this the price you and Ananias got for the land?"

After Sapphira agreed that it was, indeed, the price, Peter spoke the last words she would hear: "How could you agree to test the Spirit of the Lord? Look! The feet of the men who buried your husband are at the door, and they will carry you out also" (Acts 5:9).

With that, Sapphira died, too.

In John 4:1-26, we see a contrasting picture of honesty. Jesus met the Samaritan woman and asked her to fetch her husband. "I have no husband," she said.

"What you have just said is quite true," Jesus responded.

Jesus went on to explain what He could give her. She honestly faced her life as it was, accepted His offer to change it, and left the well a different woman.

What made the difference between Ananias and Sapphira and the woman at the well? Their approach to honesty was an outward indicator of their inward condition.

I find it easy to resist telling boldfaced lies. But as I grow in my relationship with God, I see places that need work—places where I fail to be honest with God, myself, and others. Consider the following:

"It's nice to talk to you, too." But is it really?

"I can take this one pencil from the office."

"I can use this as a write-off on my taxes. It sort of is, after all."

Several weeks ago, I picked up Courtney from school. I had discovered yet another area in my life that needed to be improved. I described the situation, and told her of my desire to make it better. As she listened, talked, and prayed with me about the problem, I hoped she was developing the willingness and ability to see weak places in her own life.

Until our children—like the Samaritan woman—realize that God sees us at our very core, they won't be truly honest. We must teach them *why* we don't break the commandments—not just *that* we don't. A group of college students I taught once said they had never been told why they shouldn't cheat, only that they shouldn't. I'm determined to give my children more.

Prayer

Revere

God, You tell us to worship You in spirit and in truth (see John 4:23). You brought light to a world lost in darkness and truth to replace the lies. How refreshing it is to know that stable, unchanging truth from generation to generation.

Release

May the words of _____'s mouth and the meditation of his heart be pleasing in Your sight (see Psalm 19:14). Whatever things are true ... noble ... right ... pure ... lovely ... admirable—if anything is excellent or praiseworthy—help _____ to think about such things (see Philippians 4:8).

Request

Your Word tells us that _____ can know the truth and it will set her free (see John 8:32). Thank You that our family is not enslaved to the bondage of lies Satan weaves around mankind. We know You, so we have the truth residing in us. Let that truth always speak loudly to _____ and reveal the lies that come her way.

Repent

I know I've been dishonest before You. Thank You for illuminating those weaknesses in me.

Recommit

We live in a deceitful world—one that exchanges a lie for the truth and deceit for integrity. But You, God, are a great discerner of hearts. ________ is Yours, and You take great joy in him as Your creation. Help ________ to feel that allegiance deep inside and abide by the truth in all he thinks and does throughout his life. Let his life be marked by integrity.

Things to Do

1. Read stories about honesty.
2. Describe a time when someone was dishonest with you.
3. Tell of a time when you were dishonest (lying or cheating) and how that made you feel.
4. Point out lies we tell ourselves, such as "I can't."

> *Deep down in me I knowed it was a lie, and he knowed it. You can't pray a lie. I found that out.*
>
> Huck Finn in *The Adventures of Huckleberry Finn*

A demanding spirit, with self-will as its rudder, blocks prayer.
Catherine Marshall

Discernment

Because I love your commands more than gold, more than pure gold, and because I consider all your precepts right, I hate every wrong path.

PSALM 119:127-28

It was payday. The Israelites had come out of Egyptian bondage and through forty years in the wilderness. The reward lay just ahead: God called it the Promised Land. But who would gain the prize and walk on in?

In Deuteronomy 32, the story unfolded. Moses wrote, "They are a nation without sense, there is no discernment in them. If only they were wise and would understand this and discern what their end will be!" (vv. 28-29).

I can feel Moses' emotions as he penned the words. Those who would cross the finish line were those who had recognized that what they see in the present can be quite different from what the end will actually be. And they chose to live accordingly. How was that played out?

The Israelites often grew discouraged. They complained and wished they were back in Egypt: "We remember the fish we ate in Egypt at no cost—also the cucumbers, melons, leeks, onions, and garlic. But now we have lost our appetite; we never see anything but this manna!" (Numbers 11:5-6).

Imagine how easy it was to join in with the complaining crowd. Imagine how difficult it was to discern the right thing and not wish to exchange the momentary pleasures of a good meal for the eternal pleasures of God's will.

All but two people went with the crowd. What payment did the crowd receive? We read about the end of one member: "Aaron died on Mount Hor and was gathered to his people. This is because ... [he] broke faith with me in the presence of the Israelites" (Deuteronomy 32:50-51).

But Joshua and Caleb chose discernment in spite of what the crowd did around them. And their payment? God said of Caleb, "He will see it, and I will give him and his descendants the land he set his feet on, because he followed the Lord wholeheartedly" (Deuteronomy 1:36).

How can we teach our children that discernment is crucial in spite of the circumstances? How can we train them to listen to its voice even when it's muted in the crowd's clamor?

I dropped Courtney off at a non-Christian friend's birthday party one day. Though I had some concerns about what she would encounter, I trusted her judgment. As I walked back in the door at home, the phone was ringing. Courtney wanted to be picked up. She told me later, "They did and said things I don't have anything in common with."

Though Courtney still sees her non-Christian friend, she does so in noncompromising settings where discernment can speak the loudest.

For parents, discernment comes from following the Lord wholeheartedly ourselves, especially when that means standing alone. Then we can claim Caleb's promise for ourselves and our children: "I will give him and his descendants the land he set his feet on."

Prayer

Revere

Thank You, Lord, that there's a right way, and You left us Your Word to show us what it is.

Release

"Listen, my son, to your father's instruction and do not forsake your mother's teaching. They will be a garland to grace your head and a chain to adorn your neck" (Proverbs 1:8-9). Secure the things _______ has learned about You since he was a child. Bring to mind the truths that will come to his rescue when he encounters tough situations.

Request

Help _______ to be a discerner of the truth, and help her to stand up for it in all circumstances. Hide the Word in her heart so she won't sin against You. Help me to be a parent who will model discernment for her and will show her how to love and learn Your Word.

Repent

I sometimes choose to roll over and get extra sleep instead of spending time with You and finding wisdom and direction for parenting. Forgive me, and help me to remember what's most important.

Recommit

As Hosea took action to redeem and protect his wayward wife, Gomer, I pray a hedge of protection around _____. Then, when Satan's temptations confront him, may he decide it's better to stay with godly choices. Give him vision always to distinguish right from wrong.

Things to Do

1. Memorize Scripture as a regular part of family devotions.
2. Allow your child to decide which movies she will see using family guidelines.
3. Surround your child with people who make moral stands in the midst of immorality.

There's nothing really consistent about human behavior except its tendency to drift toward evil.

Francis Bacon

Contemplation is nothing else but a secret, peaceful, and loving infusion of God, which, if admitted, will set the soul on fire with the spirit of love.

John of the Cross

Contentment

Godliness with contentment is great gain. For we brought nothing into the world, and we can take nothing out of it. But if we have food and clothing, we will be content with that.

1 TIMOTHY 6:6-8

Someone once said, "A happy heart is better than a full purse." Paul knew this to be so. In about A.D. 62, from his prison cell in Rome, he sent a letter to the Philippian church telling them to be satisfied *anyway:* "I have learned to be content whatever the circumstances. I know what it is to be in need, and I know what it is to have plenty. I have learned the secret of being content in any and every situation.... I can do everything through him who gives me strength" (Philippians 4:11-13).

Paul wrote these words after he had settled the issue that God is in control of all things. He realized that every good thing came from God and that, in a moment, everything could be gone. So why not rest in God's sovereignty? The alternative was to lie awake at night trying to outsmart God or to try to corral the circumstances that were out of his control. Others probably thought Paul's optimism was the product of a feeble mind and a too-long stay behind prison bars.

But Paul chose *anyway* contentment. While other prisoners in that cold, damp, dirty Roman jail fretted and fumed, Paul rolled over and went to sleep. Grandma Moses chose it, too. Artist and mother of ten children, she once wrote, "I look back on my life like a good day's work; it was done, and I feel satisfied with it. I was happy and contented ... and life is what we make it, always has been, always will be."

One Saturday afternoon, I attended Clint's basketball game. George was a member of his team. He was shorter and younger than the rest of the kids, and he lacked talent for the game. But I shall never forget his perpetual smile. This particular day, one of the bigger, better players turned to him and said, "Your shorts are a little big on you, aren't they, George?"

I turned to see George's response. Not only did his smile remain, but he tipped his head toward the boy and said, "Thank you!" as though he'd gotten the biggest compliment of the day.

George had learned to be happy in all circumstances—that *anyway* kind of contentment.

Prayer

Revere

What a comfort it is to know, Lord, that I can rest while I leave everything to Your omnipotent control.

Release

I have prayed often that _____ will be a godly person. But I also pray every day for him to be content, because "godliness with contentment is great gain." Help _____ to know that kind of contentment.

Request

I realize that teaching my children contentment begins with how I demonstrate it in my own life. Start with me, Lord. Help me, like Paul, to be satisfied and happy with what I do have, whether things are going well or badly. Then help me to teach ______ that contentment doesn't come from having more things, but from wanting less.

Repent

I confess that I've often failed to demonstrate contentment. Help me to exhibit that deep confidence that everything's OK because I belong to the One Who is the Maker of all things.

Recommit

We live in a society where the tendency is to want more, more, more. Whether that dissatisfaction stems from physical or emotional needs, help ______ to be content with everything, whether little or much, and in good times as well as bad.

Things to Do

1. Try not to complain about your lack in front of your child. Find a good accountability partner who can keep you on target in that area.
2. Teach your child songs of thanksgiving such as "Count Your Blessings, Name Them One by One."
3. Demonstrate taking needs to God together and rejoicing when the needs are met.
4. Point out well-known people who are not content though they have everything imaginable materially.

Contentment comes not from great wealth but from fewer wants.

William and Nancie Carmichael

Prayer is essentially the expression of our heart longing for love. It is not so much the listing of our requests but the breathing of our own deepest request, to be united with God as fully as possible.

Brennan Manning

Forgiveness

A man's wisdom gives him patience; it is to his glory to overlook an offense.

PROVERBS 19:11

Joseph became a slave in Egypt because of his brothers' jealousy. He could have grown extremely bitter toward them. Yet when he got his chance to confront them years later, he spoke words that left them all speechless.

"'Am I in the place of God?' he said. 'You intended to harm me, but God intended it for good to accomplish what is now being done, the saving of many lives.'... And he reassured them and spoke kindly to them" (Genesis 50:19-21).

I have a friend named Tom who is a criminal attorney, and good at what he does. One morning, after he had gotten a "not guilty" judgment for the accused in a murder case, Tom and his wife Lacey went out for Saturday morning breakfast. In the restaurant, a man and woman walked up to their table.

"Hello, we're the Temples," the woman said.

Her words startled Tom and Lacy. They exchanged pleasantries, and then the woman went on. "You just finished defending the murderer of our daughter," she said.

Tom and Lacy looked at each other, only imagining the bitterness bottled up inside this woman. Then she spoke again.

"We've been praying for you," Mrs. Temple continued, "ever since the first day the trial started. I wrote a note to my husband about you, saying, 'That man needs Jesus.' We've been praying ever since."

There will be times when, like the Temples, we find ourselves at this crossroads of bitterness and forgiveness. Our children will one day, too. We can hope our routes won't be as dramatic as they were for the Temples and Joseph, but we will face choices nonetheless.

What's the secret to responding with grace when unfairness and misfortune rock our lives? What makes people choose the high road to forgiveness?

The key is the same one needed to instill virtues in our kids, and it's only found through prayer. Jesus said, "Forgive us our debts, as we also have forgiven our debtors.... For if you forgive men when they sin against you, your heavenly Father will also forgive you. But if you do not forgive men their sins, your Father will not forgive your sins" (Matthew 6:12, 14-15).

Jesus was saying, "When you have something to forgive, take the first step toward choosing to forgive, and I will accomplish this humanly impossible response through you."

What happens if we don't take that first step? It's the one sure way to block our prayers. It places sin between us and God. It builds a wall.

We all know people dealing with unfair circumstances. Many, if not most, live the rest of their lives with a cancer of unforgiveness growing inside them. They will never know what it's like to sing in a prison cell or pray for the defender of their daughter's murderer unless they make that life-changing, prayer-releasing choice to forgive.

Prayer

Revere

Jesus hung on the cross after being beaten, spat upon, betrayed, and misunderstood. He, too, had time and reason to become bitter. But instead, He spoke the words that give hope to all mankind: "Father, forgive them, for they do not know what they are doing" (Luke 23:34). That's the example of forgiveness You left for me, God, and it's also the reason I've been forgiven of my own sins.

Release

Let all bitterness, rage, anger, brawling, and slander be put away from _____, with all malice (see Ephesians 4:31). Show _____ that this is one more way You can be strong through him.

Request

Let ______ always choose to forgive. Show her how to surrender bitter areas of her life to You. Help her to keep the lines between her and You always open.

Repent

Show me any sins of unforgiveness that lie in my heart today as I wait on You. Now forgive me and show me how to demonstrate Your forgiveness for ______.

Recommit

______ will often face the temptation to be bitter and unforgiving. I claim a tender heart for ______, free from unforgiveness and other sins that would hinder his relationship with You.

Things to Do

1. Discuss your own struggles with someone who did you wrong, as well as your choice to forgive and what that has meant.
2. Always let your child see you return good for evil, both in word and in deed. Let her see you go to God for strength in this area.
3. Memorize scriptures on forgiveness, and hold each other accountable to what those words say.
4. Model as well as teach the importance of saying, "I'm sorry."

> *When you forgive somebody who has wronged you, you're spared the dismal corrosion of bitterness and wounded pride. For both parties, forgiveness means the freedom again to be at peace inside their own skins and to be glad in each other's presence.*
>
> Frederick Buechner

Prayer is meeting the Father at His throne and from the perspective of heaven, laying all earthly matters and concerns at the feet of a sovereign God.

Kay Arthur

Reverence

The fear of the Lord is the beginning of wisdom, and knowledge of the Holy One is understanding.

PROVERBS 9:10

I looked at the bumper sticker that read, "Jesus is coming back, and boy is He mad!" My heart ached as I drove past the well-intentioned driver, who was probably thinking of himself as a real witness. *But Jesus is the One I have grown to love,* I thought. It hadn't always been that way, however.

I grew up in a Christian home, but I didn't surrender my life to Jesus until I was in my early thirties. I knew enough to be afraid of what would happen if I died, but I didn't know enough to love and revere an awesome God. As a result, I, too, imagined this really angry God, ready to zap me for letting Him down.

Then one day, I cried out to Him. I was pregnant and already had two little girls, and my husband had walked out of our lives. I had reached the end of my own strength and now needed to look to God for His. Like the prodigal son in Luke 15, I had "squandered [my] wealth in wild living" (v. 13).

Also like that young man, I decided "'I will set out and go back to my father and say to him: Father, I have sinned against heaven and against you. I am no longer worthy to be called your son; make me like one of your hired men'" (Luke 15:18-19).

So away I went, back to my Father. And while I was still a long way off, my Father saw me standing in a field, asking Him to come back into my life. He put His arms around me that September afternoon more than a decade ago. He wrapped His best robe around me and showered His love on me. He put a ring on my finger and sandals on my feet. He gave me the best He had in exchange for the mistakes I brought to Him. And He remembered my failures no more.

I long for my children never to fear God out of cowardice and timidity and shame. I want them to fall in love with Jesus in their rooms, on the basketball court, through difficult situations—any place they find Him putting His arms around them, understanding them, giving them His best, and loving them.

When that happens, reverence is born and the right kind of fear develops for this awesome God we serve.

Then when they think of Jesus, they don't see Him as really mad but as really loving, understanding, kind, and forgiving. And that will forge a lifetime relationship with Him. I'm praying like crazy that this will happen.

Prayer

Revere

"O Lord, our Lord, how majestic is Your name in all the earth!" (Psalm 8:9). I worship You with my mouth as well as my life. I love You, God.

Release

Because You are God and _____ belongs to You, he doesn't have to fear anything. Everything is under Your control. Help him to replace fear of anything else with deep love for You.

At the same time, show ______ how to fear You in a healthy way. "But the Lord, who brought you up out of the land of Egypt, with great power and a stretched out arm, him shall ye fear, and him shall ye worship" (2 Kings 17:36, KJV). Help me to remind ______ that fearing You is the beginning of wisdom in every area of his life.

Request

Help ______ to show her reverence for You through the choices she makes and the way she treats other people. "Show proper respect to everyone: Love the brotherhood of believers, fear God, honor the king" (1 Peter 2:17). Remind ______ that everything she does is to be for Your glory.

Repent

Forgive me for the times I have modeled fearing the wrong things to _____. Remind me always that I have nothing to fear as long as I'm in You.

Recommit

Help me to teach __________ that he doesn't have to fear Satan or the plans that he makes for him. Show __________ how You are greater in him than Satan is in the world. Therefore, he can walk successfully past every pitfall laid for him.

Things to Do

Find ways to teach your child godly reverence. Don't go after the disrespectful behavior she demonstrates, but pursue the beliefs that guide her. Try several things:

1. Read stories of God's overcoming power in the Bible. You can find them everywhere.
2. Contrast the people in the Bible who trusted God with those who did not. Clarify what happened to them.
3. Walk through today's choices with your child. What fears do they bring? Which of the fears are from God? Which are not?

Your glory pours into my soul like sunlight against gold.

Mechthild of Magdeburg

Epilogue

Ashley has always loved to read. When she was younger, one of her favorite outings involved trips to the Christian bookstore, where she could spend her allowance—and more when possible—on new books. When she found a really good one, she loved to share it with the rest of us. She would tell me the details of her latest read while I fixed dinner or while she and her siblings rode in the car. Once she said she wanted to read something to us. "It's the 'apology' at the back of the book," she said. I felt confused until Ashley read, and then I realized she meant the epilogue—or afterthought—in the book.

I must admit I've read some books that should have had an apology at the end, but I hope this isn't one of them. Our reason for praying for our kids is founded in God's eternal Word, and I wanted to leave you with three more reminders never to stop these prayers.

In Genesis, we read about the first instance of family intercession found in the Bible. Angels informed Abraham that God would destroy the wicked cities of Sodom and Gomorrah. Abraham's nephew Lot lived there, however, and Abraham wasted no time in pleading on behalf of this family member. As a result, Lot and most of his family walked out before the cities were destroyed.

In Joshua 2, we find another person who interceded for her family. Joshua sent soldiers to spy out the city of Jericho. A harlot named Rahab offered to help *if* they promised to spare her and her family. They did, and the family went free when the walls of Jericho fell.

We all know the story of Noah. But Hebrews 11:7 sheds light on his motivation: "By faith Noah, when warned about things not yet seen, in holy fear built an ark to save his family."

To save his family. How wonderful to know that God has made provision for the family since the beginning of time! But we're part of that provision. We must model the principles we uphold, and we must keep the names of our children ever before God. After all, like Abraham, Rahab, and Noah, we hold the key. May God be with you as you unlock the door to your child's character development.